Mental Il.......

How to Stop Panic Attacks, Mental Toughness; Helping and Preventing Anxiety Disorders and Change Your Life

By Drake Moore

Table of Contents

PANIC ATTACKS

Introduction

To understand what a panic disorder is, you must first understand the underlying psychology. It's pure fear. Fear of danger, of the unexpected, of the physical symptoms that come along, of people and of situations. The less the control of this fear is, the more severe is the disorder. Eventually people that experience this fear refuse to work, refuse to talk to other people, refuse to function, expecting that any such activity will bring about some kind of catastrophe.

The disorder is manifested by panic attacks. These may be frequent and from mild to severe in intensity. Usually the first one strikes without warning and sometimes it feels like a heart attack. In the majority of cases, the attacks last from 5 to 20 minutes, but if the disorder is more severe they can last for hours.

The body has a natural way with which to respond to danger. It is called the fight-or-flight response, which means that when there is a perceived danger, you will either have to stand and face the problem or run and hide. This response makes the heart and breath go faster and gives you a burst of energy.

The disorder manifests itself when all these things happen when there is no apparent danger and is displayed by the following symptoms:

⏹ Breathing becomes difficult

⏹ The heart is pounding or there is pain in the chest

⏹ The feeling of fear is becoming a feeling of dismay and horror

⏹ There is a feeling of choking or suffocation

⏹ Dizziness or a feeling that you are going to faint

⏹ The body is shaking or trembling

⏹ Stomachache or nausea

⏹ Sweating

⏹ Extremities are tingling or become numb

⏹ Hot flash and / or chills

⏹ A sense that all control is lost or that death is imminent

While the basis of a panic disorder is fear, there is a number of factors that may be contributing to its appearance. These are:

⏹ Hereditary predisposition

There is ample evidence that shows that panic disorder runs in families. It can pass to the offspring by one or both parents in the same way that the color of the hair or the eyes is passed.

⏹ Brain Anomalies

This refers to both physical abnormalities in some parts of the brain and mental conditions.

☐ Substance Abuse

Drugs and / or alcohol can induce the disorder. The abuse then becomes much worse.

☐ Lifestyle

A life that is very stressful or major events like the death of a loved one, loss of employment, financial bankruptcy etc... are major contributing factors to the development and manifestation of panic disorder.

☐ Medical conditions and medicinal compounds

People suffering from hyperthyroidism, heart or breathing problems and are under medication to treat these problems, can manifest panic disorders either as a result of the conditions themselves, or as a result of the medication received for the treatment of these conditions.

A common misconception of the disorder is that it is the same as agoraphobia. It is not. Agoraphobia is the fear of crowds, standing in line anywhere, going into department stores or shopping malls and fear of being unable to escape. A panic disorder may include agoraphobia but the reverse is not true.

Understanding Fears, Anxiety, Phobias And Panic Attacks

Everyone gets scared; fear is an unavoidable component of the human experience. Most of us consider fear to be a negative and unpleasant emotion, while a few of us go above and beyond to trigger it by watching scary films or even jumping out of planes.

In some cases, fear is necessary and justifiable. For example, if you hear footsteps in your house when you know that you are at home alone, your fear will keep you on high alert and probably even coerce you to hide or call the police, actions which may very well keep you from harm.

Causes of Fear

Fear can attach itself to pretty much anything, and this attachment doesn't have to be uniform in everyone. Fear can attach itself to darkness, spiders, clowns, heights, water. You name it.

In terms of evolution, we can credit fear, to an extent, for the success and survival of our species over millions and millions of years. Any organism that doesn't flee or hide in the face of danger is likely to be eliminated from the gene pool before it even has a chance to procreate further its species.

It is, therefore, a natural reflex to feel jumpy in situations that may be considered hostile. Don't you think it is better to run whenever your own shadow surprises you than to assume that you are always safe only to be attacked by another creature a few moments later? The body's physiological changes when you experience fear are often referred to as the fight-or-flight response. As the name suggests, these changes prepare you to either fight or flee.

Fight-or-Flight Response

When your body is geared into survival-mode by fear, your breathing rate increases, the heart rate spikes, your peripheral blood vessels constrict, your muscles are filled with blood, and the blood vessels around your organs dilate to feed them with larger doses of oxygen and nutrients.

Even the muscles at the base of each hair are flooded with blood and become tighter, causing piloerection, ordinarily known as goosebumps. When the hairs on a human being stand on end, it does not make much of a difference in terms of appearance. Still, for hairier creatures, I may make them appear larger and more formidable, which intimidates other animals.

When you're afraid, the levels of glucose in your bloodstream also spike, which provides a ready source of energy in case you need to take action immediately. Further, the number of white blood cells and the levels of calcium increase in the bloodstream.

At this time, the body also releases cortisol, which turns fatty acids into energy, while catecholamine hormones such as norepinephrine and epinephrine prepare your muscles for violent action. These hormones also boost activity in your lungs and heart and reduce activity in the intestines and stomach, causing "butterflies." The hormones may also inhibit the production of saliva and tears, which may explain the feeling of having a dry mouth after a fright. During all this, your pupils also dilate, causing tunnel vision, whereby you only focus on the danger ahead.

Causes of Anxious Brain

Simply put, anxiety is the apprehension or fear that puts you on high alert. Evolutionarily and biologically, anxiety is supposed to prepare us to react to potential threats.

On the surface level, anxiety may seem a lot like stress, but the reality is that it isn't that straight forward. Undoubtedly, anxiety can be a byproduct of stress, but stress can also manifest itself in other ways, including anger, sadness, or worry. Anxiety, however, is a constant feeling of dread and apprehension, even in the absence of any real trigger. Therefore, it is accurate to conclude that stress is caused by external factors, while anxiety is simply an internal response, which is why it is so much harder to control.

When you are anxious, you experience a heightened sense of awareness about every little thing that is going on around you, coupled with a deep sense of fear or dread. Before the effects manifest in your body, your brain is already heavy at work.

Studies have shown that anxiety activates the brain's autonomic nervous system responsible for the fight-or-flight response, which expresses itself through several, normally unpleasant, physiological symptoms including panic attacks, palpitations, fast pulse, chest pain, shortness of breath, headaches, insomnia, problems with speech and more.

Several parts of the brain play a key role in the production of anxiety and fear. Neurochemical techniques and brain imaging techniques indicate that the hippocampus and the amygdala play the most significant roles in anxiety disorders.

The amygdala is a little ovalis part of the brain that is responsible for processing sensory signals as well as interpreting these signals. After interpretation, the amygdala sends out signals to the rest of the brain of any perceived threats, thereby triggering anxiety or fear. There are emotional memories stored in the amygdala, which, of course, vary from person to person, thereby creating very distinct fears. For example, the fear of heights, dogs, spiders, snakes, etc.

On the other hand, the function of the hippocampus is to transform dangerous or threatening events into memories. There have been studies that suggest that this part of the brain is smaller in people who experienced childhood trauma or who have served in combat. The reduction in the size of the hippocampus has been said to be the body's attempt to reduce the role it plays in flashbacks and memories of the traumatic experiences.

Causes of Panic Attacks

Most people will experience a panic attack at least once in their lifetime, but the issue disappears once they get past a certain stressful situation. However, if you find that you have unexpected and recurrent panic attacks or that you are spending long periods in a constant state of fear, you may have to come to terms with the fact that you have a panic disorder. You should begin addressing the issue immediately.

Although panic attacks feel pretty intense, they are not life-threatening but make no mistake. They can significantly affect or downgrade your quality of life. Some of the causes of panic attacks include:

Genetics: If your family has a predisposition for anxiety or panic disorders, you are highly likely to experience these disorders yourself.

Environmental Factors: Events around you can trigger anxiety and panic. This could be stress from your job, the workings of a personal relationship, and financial predicaments. Physical stresses can also trigger panic attacks, for example, low oxygen in high-altitude regions.

Brain Chemistry: Our experiences throughout our lives can heavily influence the chemistry of our brains, and extremely traumatic or stressful experiences can alter the brain's structure, causing it to react aggressively to triggers that have caused you anxiety in the past. In fact, neurologists have described anxiety and panic disorders as the disruption of the normal workings of hormones and electrical signals in your brain.

Other Medical Factors: Underlying medical conditions can also lead to the manifestation of anxiety and panic disorders. These could be symptoms of a disease, chronic stress, and medicinal effects.

Phobias

Another huge sign of chronic anxiety is the presence of phobias. These fears have no logical roots. The victim develops an irrational dread against certain things or events. And once their fear is triggered, it stops them from functioning normally. Some of the phobias that people develop include:

1. Animal phobias

2. Environmental phobias

3. Certain situation phobias

4. Injury-related phobias

Phobia disorders are probably one of the most well-known anxiety disorders in the world. You constantly see phobias being displayed in media such as movies about clowns, heights, or spiders. Keep in mind that fear and concern regarding specific situations is completely normal and does not mean that you have a phobia. For example, if you are scared of spiders, it doesn't mean you have a phobia. However, if you revolve your life around making sure there are no spiders, then you likely have a phobia. In normal circumstances, fear is a rational and natural response in our bodies when we feel threatened.

Those who suffer from a phobia disorder will have a huge reaction when it comes to certain situations, activities, or objects. This is due to them exaggerating the danger in their heads. The terror, panic, and fear that they feel are completely blown out of proportion. In severe cases, an individual who has a phobia disorder may have a big reaction by just seeing their phobic stimulus on TV. People who have these extreme reactions often are suffering from a specific phobia disorder.

Most people who suffer from anxiety or anxiety disorders are typically not aware of where their anxiety is coming from. On the contrary, people who suffer from phobia disorder is very aware of what their fears are and how it's irrational and extreme. However, they feel like their fear is automatic and is not something that can be controlled or reduced. In serious cases of phobia disorders, it could lead to panic attacks. This increases the likelihood of this individual, also developing a panic disorder as well. The following are symptoms of a phobia disorder:

- An irrational, constant, and extreme fear of a specific situation, object, or activity. (e.g., the fear of spiders, dogs, or water)

- Constant avoidance of situations where there is a possibility of encountering a phobia. (e.g., not going outside because you may encounter a dog)

- Constant avoidance and anxiety regarding specific situations make it difficult for the individual to go about their daily routine. (e.g. not going outside because you may encounter a dog which causes you to miss important things like work/school)

- Avoidance and anxiety is constant and is lasting for 6 months +

The first symptoms of phobia disorder usually arise during childhood or early adolescence. Fear is normal throughout childhood, and children often share common fears like; strangers, the dark, imaginary monsters, and animals. However, the process of growing up is learning to manage these fears properly. Children who never learned to properly deal with their fears are at a higher risk of developing phobia disorder in their adulthood. Some children have such severe phobias that develop into panic attacks later on. This demographic has a higher chance of developing other types of anxiety disorders in their adult life.

Many different factors contribute to the development of a phobia disorder. First of all, a person's temperament and mental health history are the biggest players in the development of a phobia disorder. Fortunately, phobias are one of the more treatable disorders, and treatments like Cognitive Behavioral Therapy is the first form of treatment used to tackle this disorder. Medication will be used to treat phobia disorder in more severe cases but is likely partnered with CBT as well.

How Do Phobias Develop?

We know thus far that phobias are likely developed due to anxiety disorders. However, scientists have been studying numerous theories and have classified them into three unique categories. These include biological causes, learning-based causes, and psychoanalytic causes. It is unlikely that these causes are mutually exclusive since there is a much higher chance that these causes all interact within a person to cause the birth of a phobia. For instance, a person's cause could be the biological differences in their brain that become triggered by an experience in their environment; that negative experience they just witnessed may cause them to have a 'learned response'.

Let's take a look into three different theories.

1. Psychoanalytic Theory

This theory is based on Sigmund Freud as he pioneered the theory of the three stages of conscience within a person: These are Id, Ego, and Superego. The Id is the most instinctual aspect of the mind and is the foundation of our primitive emotions; anxiety and fear. The superego is a higher conscience that is selfless and values concepts of guilt and judgments. Lastly, the ego is there to control the Id's impulses. According to the psychoanalytic theory, phobias are created based on the Id's anxiety reactions that have been repressed by one's ego. In simpler terms, the object that is currently feared was not the original subject of the fear.

2. Learning Theory

This theory is based on a set of theories that are related to cognitive theory and behaviorism. Ivan Pavlov spearheaded the learning theory by doing an experiment that proved that dogs could be trained to salivate when a certain bell was rung. After that, other psychologists used this study to build numerous other theories based on human behavior. Based on this theory, phobias are developed when a person's fear response is punished or reinforced.

3. Biological Basis

This theory is based on a medical model of psychology. This means that this model supports the theory that phobias are caused by physiological factors. Neuropsychologists in this field have found multiple genetic factors that play a role in a person's development of phobias. This research started very recently, but it has already found that certain medications have been useful in treating one's phobias.

Many of these medical treatments work by relieving anxiety by increasing serotonin levels.

Mental Disorders And Illness

There are many types of mental illnesses; there are those that affect mood, personality, and psyche. Some of these mental illnesses, like eating disorders, can be overcome or prevented with the support of loved ones, while others require professional help. There are also critical conditions that require medication, psychiatric counselling and/or therapy.

Common Types of Mental Illness

One of the most popular, if not easily distinguishable mental illnesses, is phobia. A phobia is a type of anxiety disorder where the person afflicted has an irrational fear of an object, animal, or situation. When the person is confronted with the object of his or her fear, he or she will take great measures to keep away from it. When confrontation is inevitable, the person experiences panic attacks or feel greatly distressed.

General phobia is an irrational or unexplainable fear of the many dangers of life. General phobia is usually characterized by the fear of uncontrollable events, like death, and general threats such as natural disasters, murder, accidents, and epidemics. People with general phobia also have anxiety and tend to become restless— especially at night—because of over-thinking and over-worrying.

There are specific types of phobias that are focused on a particular object or situation, such as the fear of spiders (arachnophobia) and the fear of confined spaces (claustrophobia). Some fears are not just irrational, but also very unusual, like Tremophobia (fear of trembling), Amaxophobia (fear of riding cars), and Anthrophobia (fear of flowers).

The most common phobias are as follows:
• Arachnophobia (fear of arachnids)
• Acrophobia (fear of heights or seeing heights)
• Cynophobia (fear of dogs)
• Astraphobia (fear of thunder and lightning)
• Pteromerhanophobia
(fear of flying in planes, helicopters, etc.)

Rare Types of Mental Illnesses

Some mental illnesses are rare, but the severity of such conditions is extreme, making them infamous in the medical world. There are also psychotic disorders that don't just affect a person's behavior, but also the brain and its cognitive thinking. This type of mental illness interferes with "reality" in the eyes of the person, making him or her unable to live normally in any way. For example, schizophrenia is a condition in which a person has more than one personality and an inability to tell reality apart from fantasy.

Another known but rare condition is the infamous Manic Bipolar Disorder. People with schizophrenia develop delusional beliefs that start out as simple fantasies that later take over their lives almost completely. Sometimes, these delusions are involuntary. In addition, schizophrenics have a complicated set of behaviors and ways of thinking. Not only are schizophrenics paranoid, they may also be depressive and anxious, but in such extreme levels that they can neither think clearly, nor face choices or changes.

Schizophrenia

The main characteristics of schizophrenia are disorganized thinking, severe paranoia and/or anxiety, and a disconnection from reality. People with this condition experience hallucinations: hearing voices or seeing apparitions that are not really there. When told that these experiences are unreal, a schizophrenic might deny the truth to the extent of becoming aggressive. Schizophrenic individuals also experience phantom pains. The unreal experiences affect their way of thinking, disrupting it and leading them to disbelieve others, even loved ones.

Confusion is inevitable in this condition, and cognitive thinking is greatly affected. This kind of mental illness not only affects the afflicted person, but also the people around him or her. They are not mentally capable of doing certain jobs. It is unsafe for them to be left alone, and it is also unsafe for them to be in crowded places. People who are diagnosed with schizophrenia are considered self-destructive, and they may also pose a possible threat to others. The schizophrenic individual is not just emotionally unstable, but has no strength to control their illness, making them unpredictable and sometimes prone to inhumane actions.

There are four types of schizophrenics:

Disorganized Type - this type of schizophrenia is characterized by general disorganization. People with this type of disorder suddenly talk gibberish or recite songs, poems, or scripts, and they do so for no apparent reason. They might even invent a language of their own or simply speak out meaningless words. Some will suddenly laugh, sob, or giggle by themselves, obviously caught up and lost in their own thoughts.

Paranoid Type – paranoid type schizophrenics have extreme anxiety and fear. Their paranoia revolves around the suspicion that someone, a surreal being or secret organization, is out to capture or hurt them. A paranoid schizophrenic may also feel that others are harassing him or are scheming to overthrow, murder, or harm him in some way. People who are paranoid schizophrenic have a tendency to argue excessively with others, act aloof, and display fits of anger or rage. They have the unusual belief that there is either a known or unknown enemy nearby.

Undifferentiated Type – this type has some of the characteristics of the other types of schizophrenia. The individual may have paranoid symptoms as well as disorganization. What makes this type of schizophrenic separate is that the symptoms are not equally evident and are only transitional, if not temporary, and no symptoms are intense enough to categorize the person under a single type.

Residual Type – There are some symptoms of the condition left that may indicate a major outburst followed by complete remission, or simply no more occurrences for the rest of the individual's life.

Manic Bipolar Disorder

This disorder is infamous for its extremely noticeable characteristics. Like schizophrenics, manic-bipolar individuals have a false sense of reality and tend to live in their own thoughts of fantasy. People with this condition believe they are an entirely different person; for example, the Queen of Sheba, an ex-convict hiding from government forces, or an alien envoy from another galaxy. Their perception of reality is so altered that they have no sense of time, place, or what is happening to them. Manic bipolar individuals will suddenly act a certain way without warning, possibly hurting others. Some individuals with bipolar disorder simply stop moving or speaking for hours.

Infamous cases involve individuals talking nonsensical things, putting make-up on, and dressing in unusual ways. Some of the most serious cases involve the individual stopping in the middle of his or her activities, including walking. The person maintains this "pose" for hours without disturbance. Others may try to provoke the individual to move or speak, but to no avail. The danger in this is that the return of motion is unpredictable; it may take days before the manic bipolar resumes his activities, and sometimes when he does, he is aggressive.

Schizophrenia and manic bipolar disorder are chronic mental illnesses that require multiple medications alongside psychotherapy and moral support. Some cases take years to treat, and most individuals with these disorders experience recurring symptoms with remissions before finally achieving more stable mental health. Remissions are lingering episodes or periods of time when the afflicted individual experiences a mentally healthy state. The symptoms of their illness are absent for a time being, but the cycle ends at some point, and the onset of the symptoms returns. Not all mental illnesses have remissions; some are consistent, while other symptoms grow less in severity but are still present.

Understanding Personality Disorder

Mental illnesses vary; some are extreme and prolonged, while others are recurring but mild. Differences in consistency and severity set the types of mental illness apart from each other. Personality disorders are a kind of mental illness. They are focused on, but not specifically confined to, the behavior of the individual. While most mental illnesses have many symptoms in common, they are different by contrast and degree.

Differences Between Mental Illness and Personality Disorder

Personality disorders fall under a class of mental illness that is recognizable by patterns in human behavior. These patterns are out of the ordinary. In comparison to what most people would normally do in their culture, a person with a personality disorder feels, thinks, perceives, and relates differently. This different behavior is usually obvious, either because of its extremity in nature or lack of extremities. A person suffering from this kind of condition is capable of working and forming relationships, but with difficulty.

What is personality disorder?

Personality disorder is the condition where one's overall personality is affected by his or her thoughts and behavior. There is a pattern in the behavior that is self-destructive or dissocial in nature. Its characteristics are not acceptable to most people. The signs and symptoms begin forming during the younger years, but only become noticeable later. Signs are often evident in the workplace, where social interaction and a variety of other forces are at work, like change, pressure, and criticism. The signs and symptoms of personality disorders are much easier to see in this type of environment.

How are personality disorders obtained?

People get conditions like these during their adolescent years, when experiences are most memorable and influential. Most mental conditions are obtained during this stage. Personality disorders develop from adolescence but come to light or worsen during adulthood.

The classification of personality disorders is argued over by most institutions and psychiatric organizations because of their nature. People with personality disorder may carry the condition throughout their lives; there is a characteristic that suggests that untreated or mistreated cases grow steadily worse. People with personality disorders are also most prone to acquiring other types of mental illnesses, in addition to suicidal tendencies and substance abuse.

The Four Clusters /Types of Personality Disorder

(Clusters A & B)

Personality disorders are organized into four clusters. In each cluster, there are three to four conditions. These conditions also have subtypes with unique behavioral patterns; however, these will not be included.

Cluster A

The first cluster, Cluster A Personality Disorder, is made up of personality disorders that make an individual unable to relate to others. People with personality disorders in this cluster are usually defined as "odd," "strange," or "eccentric." They are described by others as people who seem to have a world of their own.

Paranoid

Paranoia is a condition where the person is constantly wary of his or her surroundings. Paranoid individuals generally mistrust others; some types of paranoid people will take extreme measures to ensure their safety through preparations like stockpiling food or weapons in the home. People with this condition tend to suspect bad things are about to happen; some of these fears are legitimate, while others are imaginary. One of the most extreme behaviors of paranoid people is extensively searching for evidence in their surroundings to validate their fears or suspicions. They are constantly on the look-out for signs of danger, scanning for possible escape routes in case these dangers occur. Paranoid individuals also tend to have explosive tempers; this is a defense mechanism that triggers when the individual feels apprehensive.

The causes of paranoia differ for each person. Most cases develop due to negative feelings, starting from bad parental models and leading to peer rejection and social insecurity. There are also genetic contributions to this condition. Some people with schizophrenia tend to develop paranoia and vice versa.

Schizoid

Often mistaken as schizophrenia, schizoid personality disorder is more passive in nature and not as prolonged. A person with schizoid personality disorder is distant, not only emotionally, but also socially. People with this condition are solitary and secretive. In addition to that, they are apathetic, even when it comes to social and romantic relationships. Ironically, these individuals are passive and inferior. They prefer solace because they are afraid of emotional intimacy. This disorder is rare, and some psychologists argue that its diagnosis depends on a place's cultural norms. In some countries, this type of behavior is acceptable—not necessarily normal, but not far above or below what is considered "sane."

Negligence during childhood and extremely perfectionist parenting are the main causes of schizoid personality disorders. Other causes point to genetic inheritance.

Schizotypal

Quite like the schizoid, a person with schizotypal personality disorder seeks social isolation. He or she may develop odd behaviors that others see as strange, like dressing up unusually or talking to themselves. The difference between schizoid and schizotypal is that the latter has more of an ability to converse socially, but in an odd manner, which makes it difficult for the person to form relationships. Schizotypal individuals also usually have interesting beliefs, such as those in the paranormal field.

Schizotypal traits are usually developed early in childhood. Negative experiences, such as early separation from the parents, trauma, and negligence, are major causes. Genetic inheritance is also a contributor.

Cluster B

Cluster B of personality disorders involves conditions that cause dramatic and erratic behaviors. People with Cluster B disorders have difficulty in regulating their emotions. They tend to have extreme mood swings, become overly dramatic, impulsive, and generally unpredictable. Their instability is not only visible in their emotions but is also evident in the relationships they form.

Antisocial

Antisocial personality disorder is also known as dissocial personality disorder. Antisocial individuals are seen by most as being purposefully juvenile and disruptive. They have no regard for the rights or personal space of others. Most people with antisocial personality disorder have criminal records. They seek to go in the opposite direction of what is accepted as normal. They are also prone to substance abuse and have a tendency for violence.

There are many possible causes for a person to become antisocial. The surroundings, including social influences, play a heavy role in that. Psychiatrists also consider hormonal imbalance to be a major contributor.

Borderline

Borderline personality disorder is among the most well-known personality disorders. The person with this disorder is characterized as emotionally unstable or emotionally intense. They can be impulsive or have outbursts during random situations. Unlike how normal people are, those with borderline personality disorder are more deeply in tune with their emotions. They feel more intensely, quicker, and longer than average, regardless of the situation. They are also noticeably sensitive to criticism, rejection, abandonment, and neglect.

People with borderline personality have unhealthy relationships. They put their partners in unpredictable situations, displaying extreme pleasure or extreme disappointment to their partner. This personality disorder is characterized by intense mood swings that are destructive when handled incorrectly.

Borderline individuals are usually depressed and may resort to self-mutilation during extreme emotional episodes. Being easily swayed by negative emotions coupled with an inability to handle rejection, they can be suicidal. Conversely, some might handle rejection differently, becoming manipulative to regain control of the relationship or loved one. They are especially attached to their partners when feeling alone or suspecting a lack of interest, love, or care. Self-harm is perceived by the individual as a means to end the "feeling." Most of the time, borderline individuals will "zone out" and retreat into their thoughts in an unconscious attempt to block out intense emotions.

It is widely debated as to what the main causes of borderline personality disorder are. The factors are usually complex for each patient; some have had experiences of childhood trauma or suffer from post-traumatic disorder. Others show significant environmental and social influences.

Histrionic

Histrionics basically have little to no sense of self-worth. Primarily, they dramatize for attention and seem to be playing roles most of the time. People with this disorder seek approval or praise from others, and the way they behave to acquire this attention is generally inappropriate. As attention seekers, histrionics can be overly charming, seductive, or very flirtatious. They crave stimulation and excitement, using manipulative behavior to achieve it. Their search for stimulation and excitement usually puts them in situations where they can be exploited. Since promiscuousness is also a characteristic of histrionics, the exploitation is repetitive.

Despite a lack of self-worth, histrionic individuals are ironically very mindful of their appearance and physical presentation. Oftentimes, there is egocentrism and self-indulgence involved. Apparently, the need for approval is to ensure the survival of their ego.

Relationships are very unstable and short-lived; there is an exaggeration of intimacy on the affected person's part. A mnemonic that is used to easily describe a histrionic is the phrase "Praise me," which refers to the attention-seeking and egocentric character of the ill person.

So far, there isn't enough evidence that points to how histrionic personality disorder develops. Some studies show similarities in histrionic cases involving extravagance and vanity. One of the theories of what contributes greatly to histrionic personality disorder is abnormal lustfulness. In the psychoanalysis of Freud, this lustfulness is caused by the conditional love or emotional shallowness of the parents or guardians.

Narcissistic

Narcissistic personality disorder is characterized by exaggerated self-importance. The name for the disorder is derived from Greek mythology's Narcissus, who became entranced by his own beauty (seeing his reflection in the water) and dying because of it (he never left nor stopped looking at his reflection). Narcissistic individuals feel that others are envious of them, but they are also envious of others they perceive as being better or having more than they do. Selfish, self-centered, and manipulative, narcissistic individuals are also susceptible to seek revenge when they feel they are being slighted. This makes relationships with narcissists impossible to maintain.

They may also display fits of rage or outbursts when ridiculed. They have the notion that others cannot be more right than they are. In romantic relationships, people suffering from narcissistic personality disorder are manipulative and may have a habit of keeping tabs on who's right and who's wrong. There is an irrational and unrealistic expectation of praise, admiration, and attention from others. They also talk a great deal about themselves, are arrogant, and lack true empathy for other people.

This personality disorder stems from excessive praises and admiration from parents and relatives during childhood. Children who are overvalued and overindulged are most likely to develop narcissistic personality disorder. Emotional abuse as a child and experiences of manipulative behavior in parents are also contributing factors.

Forming of Fear

The process of producing fear occurs in the brain while we are completely unaware. It starts with the terrifying stimulus that we feel and then ends with a fight-or-flight response. There are actually two paths concerning a fear response, which happen simultaneously: the low road and the high road.

The low road is rather sudden and chaotic, initiating several physiological changes including the acceleration of one's heart rate, increasing one's breathing rate and muscle tension - which can be summed up as the fight-or-flight response. This all occurs before the stimulus is identified.

The high road is more thoughtful. It takes more time in considering all options and provides a more accurate interpretation of what is really going on. It determines whether a perceived threat is real or not. It takes a little longer compared to the low road, which is the reason why unanticipated events such as knocking on the front door initially cause immediate fear, before a rational calmness settles in.

Identifying Fear

Fear isn't always considered as adaptive. A small amount of fear can serve as a motivation or encouragement in nerve-wrecking situations. It can help to sharpen the mind. On the other hand, there are several types of extreme fears that can be paralyzing or make one want to escape a situation, even when it is not the appropriate thing to do.

Once fear becomes uncontrollable, it can seriously affect a person's daily functioning. It is no longer adaptive if a person is constantly afraid of the things that haven't even occurred yet. Anxiety and panic are often the terms associated with these types of uncontrollable fears. They can have negative effects on a person's social and personal well-being.

Anxiety is a future-oriented fear. It is basically characterized by uneasiness in the mind and body, because the person doesn't have any idea of what could happen next. A person who suffers from serious anxiety attacks, struggles with the fact that they know they don't have any control over the upcoming events. To others, the fear of not having control over the future may seem silly, but it is important to understand where a person like this is coming from.

Panic is an abrupt physical response that a person experiences when there's actually nothing to be scared of. This kind of fear is often associated with phobia that can affect one's physical and emotional well-being. During a "panic attack", the person suffering may go through all kinds of physical reactions, such as shaking, grinding of the teeth, or even tapping. Again, this may seem silly to an outsider, but it is important to remember that the person suffering from a "panic attack" is literally experiencing something completely different than a "common fear".

Why Do People Fear?

One thing is for sure, if people were not afraid of anything, they wouldn't live long. They would be careless when crossing a street, careless with poisonous snakes, and may even try to freely jump off of a tall building.

Generally, fear promotes survival, and this is how we've developed so much as a species. We try things and if there is a negative result, we learn to alter our behavior or avoid that activity completely. A perfect example of this is when a small child burns his hand on a hot stove and learns to never touch it again - based on his own experience.

Have you ever wondered why people make faces when they feel terrified? Some people say that this is a way to let other people know you are afraid when you don't speak the same language as them. According to Charles Darwin, it's a result of the intuitive tensing up of muscles caused by a developed response to fear. He stated that his reason and will were defenseless against the thought of a danger that he had never experienced.

Although most people are no longer fighting to survive in the wild, fear is definitely far from being an obsolete instinct. While the media and technology in the world have helped us to develop as a species, it has also caused many fears within our culture. Many modern humans tend to anticipate dreadful things that may possibly happen to them, which they might have seen on television, read in a magazine or online publication, or heard from others on social media. However, often times these are events which will not happen to the person or are very unlikely to happen.

Ways to Overcome Fear

Fear is often considered by many in the self-help industry to be the enemy of success. Great rewards are obtained from taking risks in life. If fear often reigns within you, you'll never have the courage to take risks and you'd have a very difficult time accomplishing anything great.

Experiencing natural fear from time to time is part of life. It is a normal thing, but it can be physically and emotionally weakening if you live with constant fear. You won't be able to live your life to the fullest if you keep on refusing to join various daily activities just because you might have to face your fear of social interaction.

Even the bravest people in the world have certain fears that they have had to overcome. It doesn't really matter whether you're afraid of heights, spiders, failure, or change as long as you're courageous enough to accept, confront, and take control of your fears to keep them from restraining you, when it comes to the things you want to do most in your life.

Sooner or later, you may start to unconsciously acquire new fears, but you shouldn't dwell on them and make it a priority to unlearn those new fears as well. It's important not to deny having such fears and being aware of them is also essential, as you begin the first step towards eradicating them. Anyone can learn how to overcome fear. It's a skill. People usually just cling to them because their fears are a part of their entire disposition. There's nothing wrong if you feel like you're not yet ready to face your fears, but you will know when it is the right time. Once you've decided to start conquering your fears, here that the things that will help you accomplish your goals:

Analyze & Evaluate Your Fears

Acknowledge It

Ignoring or denying the fact that you have fears, even to yourself, is a very easy thing to do, especially when you want to appear brave or strong to others. The truth is, you can't really consider yourself as brave if you aren't able to accept the fact that you have fears in the first place.

Identify Your Fears

Sometimes fear can be easily recognized, but other times you can't even explain where those anxious feelings are coming from. Learn to name your fears. What is it exactly that makes you so afraid? Once you understand what your fears are about, you're already on your way towards eliminating them.

Journaling can be a good way to keep track of your progress while you're striving to overcome your fears. Write down every fear that bothers you. Often times when I would write down the fears that I had, I started to realize that these fears only existed in my head and the chance of the occurrence actually happening in reality was slim to none.

Identify the Structure

Dealing with your fear and considering it as something that has a beginning and an end can surely help you realize that you have control over it. Delve into its roots. When, where, and how did it begin? Did it start with a traumatic experience? Does it have anything to do with your childhood environment at school or home? How long have you been afraid of said thing? What triggers it and how does it affect you?

Fear is sometimes a healthy emotion that can protect you from harm or doing something silly. Find out whether you have a really good, realistic reason to possess this fear or if it is simply inhibiting.

Imagine Your Desired Outcome

As soon as you understand and recognize your fear, think about the things you want to change. Your main goal might be to overcome all of your limiting fears in life, but keep in mind that it is important to establish smaller, measurable goals to achieve success in the long-term.

Do it one step at a time. Imagine the person that you will be once you overcome the issues that you have right now and think about how beneficial it will be once you get there.

Take Charge Of Your Fears

Gradually Lessen Sensitivity

Usually, people are afraid of things because they haven't correctly been exposed to them. We commonly describe it as "fear of the unknown". Try to expose yourself, little by little, to the things that you're afraid of, until you learn to understand them better and your fear of them will start to dissolve.

Here is an example that you can apply to your own situation:

If you're scared of spiders, start by taking a peek at some drawings of spiders until you learn how to manage your reaction from this activity. You'll be able to notice when your body has a less visceral reaction to the drawings over time.

Eventually, you can start looking at photos of real spiders. Again, notice the feelings that arise within you at the start of this process and then see how you feel after about a week of seeing a photo of a real spider every day. If you find yourself too afraid of the change, you can simply start by gradually altering your daily routine until you find yourself capable of handling whatever life throws at you. This pattern of continually exposing yourself to slightly more fearful stimuli is often called "exposure therapy".

It is important to remember that this practice can be applied to anything that you are scared of. After you've written down your fears and admitted to being afraid of those things, you need to focus on exactly what you CAN stand. What is it that you can tolerate right now?

Do that thing. Take the little step that is in front of you right now. Tomorrow's step will be for tomorrow. As long as you expose yourself to increasingly more on a daily, weekly, or monthly basis, you're on the right track.

I want you to imagine that you are climbing a staircase and you are at the bottom right now, while the vision you have of yourself is at the top step. Take a step each day, and before you know it, you'll be approaching that top step.

Try Direct Confrontation

Sometimes, the best way to overcome your fears is to confront them, face to face. When you encounter the cause or basis of your fears, you might realize that there's really nothing to be afraid of and that you've just made up all those scary scenarios in your head. Imagination can make reality look terrifying if it gets out of control. Once you've decided to take action, your fears become weaker and the new reality isn't as bad as you'd originally thought it would be.

Learn to Handle Failure

Facing your own fears can be quite difficult and challenging, and you don't always end up triumphant right away. You may have to face them many times before you can actually say that you've defeated your fears for good. You must make it a point to remember why you started on this journey in the first place.

Focus on how helpless you'll feel if you let the fear defeat you in the long run. This thought will help to drive you when times get tough. Remember that failure is only a stepping-stone on the road to your success. The world won't end when you fail at something, but your fear will stay scary if you quit and let it be that way for good.

Don't Stop the Momentum

Typically, dealing with fear involves a great amount of momentum. You may be reading this book after a buildup of becoming frustrated with your fear. Likewise, you'll likely reach a point at which you'll be tempted to give up because of a few obstacles that you face.

Always remember that nothing is impossible when you're absolutely determined to achieve your goals. Perseverance is the key in getting past your fears. Don't worry about how much progress you made each day, just make sure that you are making progress over time. You should be trending upwards.

Let No One Stop You

There may be times when people will feed your fears and tell you that you're not good enough. Maybe they'll tell you that there's nothing you can do to change your current situation. Ignore these people and surround yourself with people who will boost your confidence and believe in your ability to overcome your challenges.

It is important to be open with others about what you are trying to overcome so that they can help you get through your struggles. It also helps to find someone who once feared what you currently fear and may have some strategies and/or tips that can be insightful for you.

Just as we mentioned earlier that negative influences can cause you to develop and maintain certain fears, the opposite is also true. You can influence yourself by listening, watching, and interacting with more positive people that encourage you. By doing so, you are stacking the odds in your favor and this is very important regarding keeping your momentum going strong.

Reach To The Common Sensation

As I've explained, the goal is never to say, "Oh, it's probably nothing" and ignore it. The goal of what you're learning is to wipe unwanted anxiety off the table, regardless of whether something is going on or not.

Here's what I mean. I was in a fully packed auditorium in the center of London during a hot summer day last year. For some reason, there was no air conditioning, and the available oxygen was dropping swiftly. My body, sensitive as it is to a lack of oxygen, warned me by raising my heart rate and by giving me a slight shortness of breath. These were symptoms I was getting because of a real issue. I didn't ignore it, because something was going on. But I chose to say, "Thanks, kind canary in the coal mine. I know there's a lack of oxygen, but I'm staying. Breathe and palpitate as you wish, I accept you." Symptoms were present; anxiety was not.

And within minutes, the feeling was gone. Because I didn't care. My body gave me a warning, one I didn't follow up upon, so it stopped warning me.

There is no way to completely avoid certain symptoms, and some circumstances may still give you a slightly heightened level of anxiety. That's normal and the goal

43

of this book is not to avoid that. As I've explained, anxiety is necessary. It's just a warning. It would be impossible to not get warnings since your body still wants you to stay alive for as long as possible. The goal is to not be intolerant to those sensations, so we don't raise unwanted and unnecessary anxiety.

Please browse through the following pages. Skip what doesn't apply to you, and read what does. You'll find some additional insights and help.

Without a doubt, the most common consequence of being prone to anxiety is:

Having crazy thoughts and believing them

You wouldn't believe the types of thoughts my mind has come up with. Well, maybe you would, because I'm sure yours has generated some crazy thoughts as well.

Thoughts that would have made me break the law had I executed them. Thoughts that would have gotten me killed had I acted upon them. Thoughts that could have made me a millionaire or, on the contrary, bankrupt. I've had them all, just as you have.

Our thought machine never takes a break, not even when we're sleeping. That's when subconscious thoughts take over.

This thought machine is a powerful ally; yet, for people who suffer from anxiety, it becomes an enemy. Something they want to shut off and eliminate.

Look, we can't ask our thought machine to just come up with positive and constructive concepts. It cannot. It

44

will come up with just about anything, from the most ridiculous to the most intelligent ideas anyone you know has ever had. And it's up to us to select what we need and discard what we don't.

Some of the thoughts will make you believe you're losing your mind; others will scare you because they will seemingly give you intentions you don't want to have.

It doesn't matter. They are just thoughts. Please let this sink in. They are just thoughts!

You don't have to agree with those thoughts, but you'll need to see them for what they are. Pieces of information.

You are not your thoughts. Having strange ideas doesn't make you weird or a bad person. This is not your will; these are not instructions that you will blindly follow. You are still in control.

You may be thinking, "Sure, Geert. But I have so many of these thoughts that I must be losing my mind." Well, please try to not think of a zebra now. Please do not think about a striped zebra running around in the sunshine eating some grass.

Aside from our thoughts, symptoms can be troublesome as well. Without a doubt, the most common symptom is:

Heart palpitations

This is the number one response to adrenaline. It's difficult to have anxiety and not have it affect your heart. I had a tendency to place my finger on the vein in my neck, just to measure the status of my heart. If my heart was doing anything other than beating slowly, I'd panic even more and start the vicious cycle discussed in the beginning of this book.

We cannot really control our heart. Sure, our thoughts can help it calm down or speed up a bit, but if there ever would be a serious problem with our heart, our thoughts wouldn't be able to fix it.

The heart has many reasons to beat faster other than you being physically active. If you drink alcohol, your heart will beat faster since alcohol is a poison to our bodies. If you're sick and your immune system is fending off a virus, your heart will beat (a lot) faster. If you've eaten an ingredient you're allergic to, your heart will beat faster too. Nothing bad is going on then, your body is simply doing its job.

Irregular heartbeats are no source of concern either, provided your doctor confirmed you are healthy heart-wise.

Since overcoming my panic attacks, my approach truly has always been to just let my heart do what it wanted. For fourteen years, I thought I was going to die right then and there at least once per week. I now decide I prefer to die once, for real, instead of in my own imagination multiple times a week. I want to truly live in the mean time.

Good ways to deal with heart symptoms are to just accept them, to say, "Whatever happens, it's OK. If it's something bad, I'll deal with it then but now I'm still standing." Use the friend method and comfort yourself. Or push harder and say, "Is that all you've got? Beat faster!" Reconfirm that you're sick of being scared. You can also finally embrace it, letting the feeling of fear wash over you. Feel it, instead of frantically pushing it away like you probably used to.

Pick anything you like or a combo of everything, combined with the other techniques you've gotten on the menu in part two. Your heart is always going to mind its own business. We better let it.

This is indeed mostly a trust issue. Anxiety will only rise when you don't trust your heart to do the right thing. That's what the "what if?" thoughts will try to tell you. If they don't, your negative radio will most probably be adding, "Yeah but you know you're probably having a heart attack." To which my reply has become, "Whatever. Whatever happens it's OK, even that." This was just my way of making fun of it and of accepting the anxiety. I, of course, preferred not to die!

I've been explaining how to use this sentence for over a decade to the people who followed the audio course, and the results have been nothing less than amazing. So give this a try, as hard and ridiculous as it may sound at first. I, personally, only worry if my heart doesn't beat at all. And that has so far never happened.

Red face

This is a great one if you suffer from a social phobia. There you are, minding your own business while sitting or standing in a public setting, possibly in conversation with someone else and suddenly you feel the wave of warmth entering your face. You know what that means... your skin will start to look red in no time, that or sweat beads will start to form, mimicking the

Niagara waterfalls on your forehead. And if they don't start on your face, they may do so in your arm pits before going for a collective run down your shirt.

A red face, flushing, and sweating are very common and normal during slight to moderate anxiety. A true panic attack, however, will probably give you a pale face, given that your blood will mostly rush to your muscles then. During moments of regular anxiety, however, the blood will rise to your head because that's where our brain tends to be. It needs oxygen and blood to operate well and find a way out of the possible predicament your amygdala believes you to be in.

Here too, pure acceptance is key. You can use any of the techniques mentioned in part two.

I like humor as a technique, with sentences like, "Other people have to pay to go to a sauna. I have one built in." And when someone notices your red face and comments on it, instead of feeling ashamed, state, "Yeah, well, you know how chameleons can change color? I've been practicing and practicing, but for now it only works with the red tone."

This form of anxiety can only hurt you socially when you let it, when you consider it as a weakness. It isn't. It's just a symptom. When you're hot, you sweat and get a red face. And sure, other people may not be feeling hot, but you are.

Fear of driving

This is a very common fear for a variety of reasons. In my home country Belgium, people who have a fear of driving are scared of all of the lunatics driving around on the roads. If you ever drive on a Belgian highway close to Brussels, you'll see that a lot of drivers go well over the speed limit and seem to love driving bumper to bumper.

In France, most of my clients with a fear of driving are afraid they can't get off the highway when they want, because there are areas of hundreds of miles without an exit on well-fenced toll roads.

In the US, the many lanes on most highways give some people the creeps. And in every country, I encounter people with a fear of:

- bridges
- tunnels
- driving too far away from home
- stop lights
- traffic jams
- trucks and big rigs
- speed
- getting involved in an accident
- causing an accident
- losing control
- losing their mind while at the wheel

Their mind comes up with dangerous scenarios out of nowhere. Collisions, causing a collision, fainting, no longer trusting the fact that they can control the car at all times and more.

Do these people have proof that all of the bad things their mind games come up with can indeed happen?

Sure, it happens all the time in movies like Die Hard, The End of the World and Godzilla. In real life, these accidents aren't so frequent.

And even if some of the scenarios they fear are realistic, these people are still causing the anxiety all on their own, considering they are not in that precarious situation they're vividly imagining.

I've met people who were involved in actual, major car crashes, who spent time in the hospital for weeks and now still drive, without anxiety.

So here too, there's more at play than the actual location or the activity of driving. It's the anxiety we are adding by believing and following our thoughts and the many what-if scenarios they will serve. That's the true cause.

Why would the mind do this?

It has to. Driving is unnatural. There you are, driving around at speeds you could never ever run at, getting sensations both visually and physically that your body doesn't recognize as natural. Because of this, your radar is put on high alert. It is dangerous.

That's why, when you learn to drive, driving feels scary. The fast movement that your body senses and the many visual stimuli (other cars for one) that you need to take into account are strange and impressive. For most people, however, the confidence they gain by not crashing and by seeing other people drive around too, conquers this fear. They gain trust, and the amygdala and other alarm systems relax.

For some, this trust never came, and they fail to ever feel at ease. For others, that confidence gradually declines as they age or quickly deteriorates after a traumatizing experience.

When it happens later in life, it's just because the radar that handles all of the visual stimuli is having a much harder time to process everything because our brains slow down a bit with age. The danger radar consequently becomes much more sensitive.

You may have noticed that older people drive slower; they just need more time to process everything that happens at certain speeds.

This, of course, is not a reason to avoid driving. If you feel that your danger radar becomes more alert, thank it, and use any of the techniques discussed in part two to soothe yourself. There is no increased danger.

Life simply is dangerous. You are able to accept this perfectly well in most areas of your life, and it should be accepted while driving as well. Especially so because you are a good driver. Your alertness and danger radar make you a better driver!

Who are the ones causing the most accidents? Drunk people. People on their phones. That's because their alertness and danger radar is at sub-zero levels at that time.

Please remember this insight and repeat it to yourself should you start to see driving as dangerous. It's just your danger radar, and that's exactly the one that's keeping you safe. Compliment it, accept it, and let go.

For some people, the fear is different. They fear not being able to get out, losing their minds and causing an accident themselves, getting and staying stuck and so on.

Let go.

"Whatever happens, it's OK. I give up, I embrace, I accept, so be it!"

I won't repeat everything I explained in part two, but remember that even though some of the possible outcomes would not be OK, accepting them and ridiculously thinking they are fine is always better than ridiculously thinking there's a high probability the bad thing is going to happen. Always choose the path of no anxiety. You're fine, you're always fine, you always have been fine. And even when something bad happens, as the great Victor Frankl would say, you can choose to be fine.

The jolt of adrenaline and the weird sensations can be a bit harder to deal with while driving, because your body wants to run and move, and yet you're sitting strapped in in your unmovable car seat.

What works well here is to start singing loudly or yelling YIHA to use up some of the adrenaline. It's just excitement because you're doing something that your body considers exciting.

And let's face it, it is. Can you imagine how a cavewoman or caveman would have responded had we put them in the back seat of a car doing just thirty miles an hour? They would have been in shock and awe.

As you practice dealing with your fear of driving, you can take baby steps. You can go for practice runs at a quiet moment or jump into the deep end of the pool and drive in the middle of rush hour traffic. It's up to you.

Also know that it's totally fine if you have to stop and park the car to take a minute to calm down. Everything is OK, no matter how you choose to deal with it.

When you practice, be proud! If you made it ten yards or ten miles, it doesn't matter.

And I mean that. If you suffer from a fear of driving, it's important to make it less important, to make it matter less. Just do it, go with the flow, and accept what you will feel. The more you can do that, the sooner the fear will start to subside.

Fear of flying

This is one of my favorites. Getting into an airplane with over a hundred people and not being able to get out for hours. That and who knows what happens when someone forgot to securely attach the wings to the plane...

You wouldn't believe the kinds of disaster scenarios my mind came up with while flying. I'm sorry, of course you would, you're probably experiencing many of those very same mind games as well.

With a fear of flying many danger radars will sound the alarm. First, there's a change in the oxygen levels on board as soon as the doors close. We're no longer breathing in pure, natural air, and the body senses it. For some people, me included, this will sound an alarm. It's the "get out of the coal mine" alarm that can launch a pounding heart, shortness of breath, nausea, possibly some vertigo, and a general feeling of malaise and discomfort.

This alone can be enough to act as a first trigger and launch the vicious panic cycle I discussed in the beginning. Don't let it, and just explain to yourself what's happening and why. It's just your body trying to warn you that you may need to pay attention and that something dangerous may be going on. When it does, it's always up to us to decide whether it is or not. And in this case, we all know flying is one of the safest ways to travel and that you're not going to fall without oxygen.

Actions Against Anxiety

It may seem elementary for you to create an action plan when it comes to your anxiety. This doesn't make you a weak person, either. We make plans for emergencies with our families. There are drills at schools and our workplaces for fires and tornadoes. Why shouldn't we have a plan that we practice for our anxiety disorder? This is something that is an emergency for someone with anxiety, and it is important to include those around us with our plan when an emergency arises.

This can be done on paper or mentally. Starting out, it is probably better to have it down on paper so that everyone around you can understand what you need and how you are feeling. Start by assessing your anxiety level. Give it a number from zero to ten. Zero is no anxiety, and ten is a full-on anxiety attack. Have a plan in place for various levels of anxiety. Make sure those around you know when it is time for you to seek medical attention.

Make sure your plan includes the number for your physician and that there are people you are around a lot authorized to discuss your situation with this provider.

If you aren't utilizing a paper plan, make sure your physician's number is clearly labeled on your phone. It wouldn't hurt to make them one of your ICE (In Case of Emergency) contacts. If you have been dealing with anxiety for a while, there is a good chance that you and your physician have a good relationship, and they can talk you through it without an office visit immediately.

Don't try to hold in your anxiety, either. Keeping it from people around you can only make the situation worse. It could simply be something that you needed to take a ten-minute break to walk away from what triggered you, but you were too proud to admit that you needed help. It is okay to ask for help. At some point in every person's life, we have to ask for help in some way or another. This just happens to be what you need help with, and having someone cover you for an extra ten-minute break so that you can catch your breath is not a crime.

Keep a notepad or a word document (if you cannot have paper at your desk) close by so that if you start feeling overwhelming feelings, you can write them down. They don't have to make sense, and often times when you go back and read what you have written after the feeling passes, you can learn from it. Sometimes our minds overreact to situations when they didn't need to. That doesn't mean that this wasn't something that truly affected you; it just means that you need to work on coping mechanisms for it. Nobody can tell you what anxiety plan is right for you. You are the one with the most knowledge about your feelings. You may have even come up with special tricks over the years to help you self-regulate, and that is something that you should write down in your plan.

How To Treat Panic Attacks

Treatment Option and Drug Therapy

When an individual is suffering from any anxiety disorder, they can have extreme symptoms that may affect many aspects of their life and find it overwhelming.

Cognitive Behavioral Therapy has been proven to help overcome the more extreme aspects of Separation Anxiety and Obsessive-Compulsive Disorder and can help with changing negative thought patterns and redirecting response behaviors. The core aspect of anxiety response behaviors is developed in early childhood as a response to trauma and were responses that were created for protection and defense reasons. These behaviors of self-isolation and the pattern of over-worrying and internal criticism are knee-jerk reactions to any situation that feels uncomfortable such as loved one leaving for a trip, and have the potential for what we may perceive as danger such as sickness from drinking out of a cup that hasn't been cleaned properly. They fear their reception by others, judgment, and making a mistake that will have dire repercussions. Their internal self-talk is full of criticism and judgment or harsh reminders of times they have failed to be understood or fit in with others. When someone is suffering from anxiety, they will argue themselves out of attending events or joining in social activities. Without much conscious consideration, they will decline to join in a group, explore a new experience or meet new individuals their minds throw up roadblocks before they even attempt social interaction. They have a knee-jerk reaction to any new circumstances and will seek to isolate themselves from meeting new people or trying new things due to their fear of failure, low self-esteem, or lack of self-confidence. Their lack of self-worth and insecurities hold them back from making the personal connections they want and need in their life. These self-sabotaging behaviors can be changed by altering the neural pathways in the brain through Cognitive Behavioral Therapy.

This is addressed in Cognitive Behavioral Therapy in a few ways the first is by determining the "meaning" that someone with Social Anxiety Disorder, Obsessive-Compulsive Disorder or Separation Anxiety attributes to circumstances. In the case of someone who is suffering from Separation Anxiety the meaning of "fear" and "abandonment" is attributed to their separation from their loved one. They apply the definition of "harm" or "unsafe" to the distance between themselves and their loved one, fearing that something will happen to their loved one or that they will suffer from some calamity if they are apart from their loved one. In this circumstance, the therapist may introduce a new thought process to the patient to redefine the distance as a normal life experience and create an internal script that sets about self-comforting and reassuring them that all is well. The therapist may have them walk through an imagined disaster scenario that has the patient feeling insecure or unsafe and create a new story where they feel sure of themselves and secure in every activity that they may encounter while apart from their loved one. In the case of an individual who is suffering from Obsessive-Compulsive Disorder, the therapist may direct the patient to describe what feeling or fear they attribute to not counting out loud all of the steps that lead up to their home. The patient may describe having a sense of "bad luck" or "disorder" to not taking the time to engage in this daily repetitive behavior. In this instance the therapist may have the patient visualize a different outcome to their not counting that has a positive impact on their breaking the habit such as walking up the stairs quickly without counting results in their favorite television episode or meeting their neighbor before they take their dog for a walk and having a pleasant conversational exchange. In this particular attribution behavior, the therapist will encourage the patient to re-frame their fear by superseding the outcome scenario to have a positive result to divert their thinking from the fear-based scenarios or superstitious behaviors they are currently enacting. By creating a new story in the mind of the individual who is suffering an anxiety disorder Cognitive Behavioral Therapy creates new thought process in the neural pathways that are focused on optimistic or positive outcomes, which over time and with diligent practice will become the preferred way of thinking for the patient.

Another component of Cognitive Behavioral Therapy is the "The Pyramid of Adaptive Exposure," where the therapist will encourage the patient to take "baby steps" in correcting their behavior. It is through the act of performing one or two tasks each week that the patient fears that they begin to overcome their anxiety disorder. As they tackle each "level" of fear-based activity the patient begins to experience success and overcome the attributed meaning of "danger" and "mistakes" occurring with these actions. As the individual who suffers from Social Anxiety Disorder takes small steps each day to initiate conversation with their colleagues or neighbors or goes to the local department store to do their shopping instead of using an online retailer they begin to realize that there is no judgment from the clerk at the store or become aware that there is no danger of confrontation with another customer on the same check-out line. If the person who is suffering from Obsessive-Compulsive Disorder is guided by the therapist to slowly begin to check the lock only once when they go to bed or turn off an appliance when leaving their home just once without returning they begin to trust themselves and have confidence in their self-awareness while detaching from these repetitive behaviors has the added bonus of showing them they are "safe" in the world and capable of taking care of themselves. When the person who suffers from Separation Anxiety begins to take the small steps of ceasing to call their child's school to check if they are okay, and the child returns home safely they realize their dark thoughts are just that and can begin to look at the world as a less violent and dangerous place for their little one to be living in. This aspect of Cognitive Behavioral Therapy is to begin to with small steps to conquer each aspect of the patients' anxiety and with each success the individual who is suffering from anxiety will begin to build new thought processes that will build new neural pathways that are designed to break them out of their avoidance or safety habits. With time the patient will develop a whole new frame of thinking that encourages and inner dialogue that encourages them to feel safe, confident, and secure in situations and activities that once brought on anxiety.

Other aspects of Cognitive Behavioral Therapy employed may be the use of role-play where the therapist may play a role of the supervisor with a person who suffers from Social Anxiety Disorder and encourage the patient to speak to them in the context of asking for a raise or addressing their desire to have an updated software program to perform their job better. In this particular dynamic, the therapist will be the "stand-in" for the employer and encourage the patient to speak with confidence and clarity regarding their needs without fear of repercussion or judgment. In some cases, the therapist may have the patient engage in group therapy if they suffer from shyness to assist them in learning how to navigate the social dynamics of a group in scenarios that mirror social occasions. in these group sessions, everyone is encouraged to use social tools that have been practiced initiating conversation and present themselves confidently. By using role-play therapy in this context and setting the person who is suffering from anxiety learns the value of presenting themselves with confidence and gains valuable social skills that can be applied naturally to real-life situations.

The overall goal of Cognitive Behavioral Therapy is to encourage the patient to change the stories that they are telling themselves regarding the possible negative outcomes of certain situations and circumstances if they do not employ their avoidance and self-protective behaviors. The therapist will work with the individual each session to slowly redirect their frame of mind when it comes to approaching new situations and engaging with new people to build their confidence through repetitive counter behavior that encourages them to open up to new experiences and reinforce their ability to navigate these scenarios successfully. In many instances, the patient becomes clear on what is merely thought, brought upon them through insecurity and negative inner dialogue, and will learn to adapt the new patterns of behavior with ease bringing enrichment to their life.

With an individual that is suffering from Separation Anxiety or Obsessive-Compulsive Disorder, there may roadblock to overcoming actions that are associated with safety or thinking processes that are compulsory and cannot be re-directed through exploratory role play or breaking a repetitive behavior. As we have mentioned earlier there is a break in the frontal cortex of the brain and cognitive activity when a person is suffering from this type of anxiety. When it is compulsory thought processes that are bringing on the anxiety or compulsory behavior in a patient and other therapy options have been explored and have had little result then the introduction of medication may prove to be beneficial in advancing therapeutic methods. There are a few medications that have shown to be helpful when combined with Cognitive Behavioral Therapy in breaking through especially difficult compulsory or anxious patterns of behavior and thought process. we will list a few of them below. It is suggested that you speak with your health care provider about taking this or any medication in combination with therapy if you feel that you are suffering from some of the extreme symptoms of one or more of the anxiety disorders mentioned in this book.

Selective Serotonin Reuptake Inhibitor (SSRI) and Serotonin/Noradrenaline Reuptake Inhibitors (SNRI)

Selective Serotonin Reuptake Inhibitors or SSRIs and Serotonin/Noradrenaline Reuptake Inhibitors or SNRIs have been proven to be effective in activating the amygdala, which controls fear and anxiety. By blocking the fight or flight response in a patient they are better able to cope with situations or activities they find intimidating which enables them to work through "The Pyramid of Adaptive Exposure" and gain the exposure and experience necessary for them to adapt to everyday circumstances and overcome anxious, avoidance and compulsory behavior.

A few common Selective Serotonin Reuptake Inhibitor (SSRI) medications you may want to discuss with your healthcare provider, or therapist are:

Citalopram

Brands: Celexa

How it works: Helpful for depression, panic disorder, social anxiety, obsessive-compulsive disorder, generalized anxiety, and PTSD.

Escitalopram

Brands: Lexapro

How it works: Helpful for generalized anxiety disorder, social anxiety disorder, PTSD, and depression.

Fluoxetine

Brands: Prozac

How it works: Helpful for depression, panic disorder, social anxiety, obsessive-compulsive disorder, generalized anxiety, and PTSD. Current research suggests some benefits for social anxiety.

Fluvoxamine

Brands: Luvox

How it works: Helpful for depression, panic disorder, social anxiety, obsessive-compulsive disorder, generalized anxiety, and PTSD.

Paroxetine

Brands: Paxil

How it works: Helpful for depression, panic disorder, social anxiety, obsessive-compulsive disorder, generalized anxiety, and PTSD.

Sertraline

Brands: Zoloft

How it works: Helpful for depression, panic disorder, social anxiety, obsessive-compulsive disorder, generalized anxiety, and PTSD. Low level of nervousness or agitation as a side effect.

A few common Serotonin/Noradrenaline Reuptake Inhibitors (SNRI) medications you may want to discuss with your healthcare provider, or therapist are:

Desvenlafaxine

Brands: (Pristiq, Khedezla)

How it works: These medications work by reducing the brain's reabsorption of the chemical serotonin and norepinephrine.

Duloxetine

Brands: (Cymbalta) – also approved to treat anxiety and certain types of chronic pain

How it works: These medications work by reducing the brain's reabsorption of the chemical's serotonin and norepinephrine.

Levomilnacipran

Brands: (Fetzima)

How it works: These medications work by reducing the brain's reabsorption of the chemical's serotonin and norepinephrine.

Venlafaxine

Brands: (Effexor XR) – also approved to treat anxiety and panic disorder

How it works: These medications work by reducing the brain's reabsorption of the chemical's serotonin and norepinephrine.

It should be noted that these drugs are psychoactive, and it will take time for the body and brain to adapt to the positive effects. Be sure to speak with your therapist and continue your treatment before stopping these medications once you have begun a treatment program. Most patients have expressed seeing results after 4 - 6 weeks of treatment, but as each person's biochemical physiology is different, you may experience different results. Be sure to work in unison with your healthcare provider and therapist to track your body's adaption of any treatment program you begin.

Realizing Control

Our minds are a blank from birth, and as we grow, we start to form a mindset based on our experiences and the kind of thoughts we allow to thrive in there. So, the first step you can take toward restoring your sense of emotional intelligence and fighting off anxiety is to be in control of your mind, emotions, and internal thoughts.

Most people who have struggled with anxiety will tell you that when they look back at their experience, they remember the exact thought that triggered the anxiety. However, because they didn't take action, it lingered on until it created a big problem for them.

Being aware of your emotions and how you feel at the very moment is a significant part of being emotionally intelligent, and it is also a crucial step toward laying off anxiety. But there is something better than awareness: control!

You need to become proactive with taking control of your emotions and not allowing anything negative to settle into your mind. We feel "strange" when someone says something unpleasant to us or when we don't know whether we will get the job we applied for or get rejected. However, what we do afterward is what counts.

You may not be able to control what everyone else does to you, but you can control how you respond to it from the inside because that is what matters. There may be specific anxiety triggers that are always with you. Maybe certain places make you feel less of yourself. Well, what are you going to do about it?

Some of the hallmarks of being emotionally intelligent are the ability to take action when necessary, especially with issues that affect your mental health, and this is where control is required. If you are not taking charge of how you feel or how others make you think, then you will be building up an emotional imbalance in your life.

But how do you control something you don't have any awareness about? It begins with being aware and then curtailing the effect it has on you by taking control. For some people, it isn't the events in their lives that cause anxiety; it is the people they interact with.

But why will anyone continually spend time with people who make them feel anxious? Although quite shocking, some people do not do anything about toxic persons. Their continued interaction with such persons creates a very negative impression in their minds that will increase their anxiety level.

Someday, such persons will discover that they are slowly sliding into depression because they tolerated and accepted toxicity that made them anxious for too long. Your internal thoughts are like the dialogue you have with yourself, and unfortunately, what you say to yourself often might be the kind of words you've repeatedly heard over time.

Take control of your internal thoughts by being mindful of what people say to you. If you don't like a word being used on you repeatedly, make it clear to the individual(s).

Words that are spoken to you are like seeds that germinate into emotions in mind, thus creating a mindset for you. That mindset will form a vital part of your character/attitude, which also affects the way you relate with others.

Now I know there are some unusual cases where you may say you don't have control over what a person says to you (for instance, the person is your boss or senior to you in some way). However, this isn't true. The fact that a person is older than you shouldn't be a reason why you can't take control of your emotional responses.

If someone who leads you makes you feel anxious all the time, you need to control the narrative by politely stating that you don't want to be spoken to in that manner. In addition to speaking up, you can also create a defense mechanism that enables you to protect yourself from such a person.

The defense mechanism may entail you ignoring the wrong comments or completely blocking them off your mind entirely. These are options you can implement, and the possibilities are better than not doing anything at all.

If you are reading this book because you want to help someone else who is going through this struggle with anxiety, then you have to be a kind of accountability partner for this person by ensuring that they are taking control of their mind and emotions.

Because you are helping this individual, you will need to commit to the process as you are dealing with someone else, and they may tell you they're all right and not be. So, you will have to continually check on the person, help them build emotional intelligence, and get them to become comfortable with their emotions enough to want to protect it from discomforting situations.

Anxiety doesn't happen spontaneously; it builds up from one incident/event to another, which is why being in control is so crucial because you will be dealing with the problem from the roots and cutting it off entirely instead of tolerating the process and "hoping" that one day you will be fine.

The connection between emotions, mindset, and internal thoughts will be easily broken when you are no longer in control of what happens to and around you. So, one day, you feel great, and within seconds, your internal thoughts are negative because you've suddenly become anxious.

There will be a lot of disparity between what happens around you and how you feel. This occurs when you don't have control over your life through your emotions and the relationship you have with other people.

We have to begin with this first idea because it is so crucial. Without control, you cannot attain new heights with emotional intelligence, and without restriction, anxiety will always be a challenging experience for you.

But it doesn't end with being in control. Control is like the first step to take because you need to reclaim your life. After taking back your life, what happens next? You become expressive!

Find Your Safe Zone

This is no way to live, and the fact that you're reading this book shows that you don't want to continue to live that way. An anxiety disorder is a common occurrence in today's modern world. Things move fast, and the ability to take your time and relish at the moment is fleeting at best. However, it is comforting to know that you don't have to live that way. You can do something about it.

Google anxiety, and you will be immediately inundated with options of all kinds. Some will promise to heal you through herbs and diets, others offer you a wide array of medications, and then some will tell you just to slough it off, and things will get better. You and I both know and understand that your choices for reclaiming your life are many.

While there has been a great deal of success in many of these methods, we encourage you to attempt to resolve your anxiety issues in a more natural way. Your brain and your body have already been designed to heal itself. It's just that most of us have lost touch with how to communicate with our bodies effectively. We go through life like an automaton, jumping from one function to another, void of feelings and confidence. However, if we learn to tap into our own natural resources, health and recovery are often just a short distance away.

The reality is that we have the power to heal ourselves within us. In most cases, you won't need expensive medications, pay hundreds of dollars to therapists, or buy into a lot of expensive gadgetry. There are steps you can take right now, techniques you can apply the moment you feel your anxiety start to rise to help your mind to reach a calmer state so you can add more positive feelings to your life.

Getting in the Right Frame of Mind

Regardless of the method, you choose to aid you in recovery, keep these basic points in mind before you begin any treatment. We live in a world full of negativity, so it's no wonder that we drift off into the negativity of land without effort. The challenge, though, is to redirect our thoughts to the more positive. This will be the first step in getting our thinking back on track.

Show Gratitude: Cultivate a spirit of gratitude.

Believe it or not, this is a mental exercise that all of us can practice. This is not just to be thankful for the basic things in life but to think deeper in that same line of thought. Making a concerted effort to at least feel gratitude inside can start us thinking more positively.

Our world is rushed, and often, we don't take the time to appreciate the things we receive without asking. Good health, a family that cares, a regular paycheck, or just being able to have a meal on the table. In the beginning, you may have to set up reminders to stop and show your appreciation for what you have.

We are all accustomed to using cues to remind us of other activities, so it just makes sense that we would use similar cues to remind us to think on more positive lines. You do this enough, and eventually, your mind will start to do it automatically, without thought or planning. Sometimes, we do this without noticing. For example, if you know you're going in to work with a very demanding boss, you mentally prepare yourself. You walk in with a spirit of wariness, and you've thought of everything you can think of to help you get through the day smoothly. You do the same if you plan to visit a sick friend. The same should also be true when you are preparing for a potential anxiety attack. The more you prepare your mind ahead of time, the easier it will be when you are actually working to push that anxiety back down to a level where it belongs.

Reject Your Inner Sensations:

Next, you want to recognize those negative thoughts and refuse to accept them. A gift is not a gift until you accept it. So, if your mind is flooded with negativity, realize that you have the option to say no to it. You are not compelled to accept any thought or feeling just because it came from your subconscious mind.

Our subconscious mind has been trained by our myriad of experiences that we go through from the moment of birth. Sadly, we have often forgotten the experiences that led to our negative thinking, and only the thoughts remain. Just as we said earlier in this book, change is a natural part of life, and any experience you had that shaped your negativity and fears most likely no longer exists. Learning to say no to such things will help you stabilize your mind and put you in a more positive perspective.

Find Your Safety Zone:

No matter how bad we think something may be or has the potential to be, it is always easier to handle when we know that we have a safe place to run to. Our safety zone doesn't always have to be a physical place to hide. It can be a form of meditation or just a mental state you train your mind to run to when things get to be too much.

Because of the crazy world we live in, most of us have forgotten how to live. We are constantly on the watch, focusing our attention on potential dangers, threats, malice, and pain. When we fall into that line of thinking, we feel everything is not safe. Start making it a habit to look for the good things in your life. They are there, hidden away behind a wealth of badness, but you can find them. You just have to look for them.

Change Your Inner Critic:

We all have that inner voice that is constantly reminding us of our past failures and our faults. This is not a characteristic exclusive to those with an anxiety disorder. It is common to all of us. But we have to start making a concerted effort to put that voice on mute. Those harsh words were drilled into us years ago, possibly when we were children and couldn't do everything right. But now, we have to change that dynamic. Up until this point, it has been a one-way conversation with that tiny voice buzzing all these negatives in your ear. It's time for you to start talking back to it.

Our inner critic acts like a judge that has nothing good to say. It judges the quality of our work, predicts how other people will view you, and makes you feel guilty and ashamed at every turn. It mocks you, teases you, and bullies you. He doesn't care about your feelings and has only one goal, and that is to prevent you from having any joy in life by questioning and doubting everything you do.

A Word at the Right Time

Another mystical tradition that has done wonders to help relieve anxiety is the use of affirmations. Because you're caught in a loop of negative thinking that has undoubtedly taken its toll. The use of positive affirmations is a great way to interrupt those negative thoughts with something positive verbally. It aids your mind to shift its thinking and gradually guides the mental process in another direction.

You can use these affirmations in three different ways.

•You can say them silently to yourself.

•You can write them down.

•You can say them out loud to yourself.

Anytime you feel overwhelmed with negative thoughts, and you can use these positive affirmations to redirect your thoughts in a more positive direction. Some therapists recommend that you make it a habit by attaching your affirmations to something you do every day. For example, every time you get in your car, you repeat your affirmations. Or you could say them every time you go to prepare a meal, put your children to bed, or hang up the phone. The trick here is to make it a regular habit to use these affirmations until they become a natural habit to you.

Some examples of positive affirmations you could make to fight off anxiety:

•I am calm.

•I am a good person.

•I value who I have become.

•I am healthy.

•I feel relaxed.

•I can let go of this stress.

•I am a good student.

•I can make a new friend today.

•I have a good relationship with my family and friends.

There are some basic rules about creating your own affirmations. First, all affirmations must be used in the present tense. Do not make mantras about the future or refer to something in the past. Second, they must always be about you. You are battling your own inner thinking process; therefore, your affirmation should be there to redirect your thinking. This is the only thing you have any control over. And third, they have to be 100% positive. Do not use any words like can't, don't, won't, etc. Instead of saying I can't get angry anymore, rephrase it to say, "I am going to stay calm today."

Many people question the value of something as simple as positive affirmations. However, while they are not an actual cure for an anxiety disorder, they are a powerful coping technique that will work for you until you can get the benefit of more long-term treatment options. You can think of them as a means to counteract those negative thoughts while you are working on something else. They are there to give your brain an alternative way of thinking.

While they are commonly used when negative feelings and thoughts pop up, some have found they do better if they start their day with affirmations, letting them start on a more positive note.

However, you choose to use them; they can help ease your anxiety in many ways:

•They are a positive distraction and can keep your thoughts from running wild.

•They give you a positive belief. In time, the brain will adapt to the positive phrases and start to adapt to the belief that you are trying to form.

•And they serve as a constant reminder to insert more positive things in your life.

Make sure that the affirmations you choose have personal meaning to you. While you can find a long list of suggestions online, one that you create yourself will have more influence over your thinking than something written by a total stranger.

You need to be committed to using them regularly. It may take time before you begin to see the benefits, but if you continue, eventually, you'll start to feel the anxious discomfort fade away replaced by something more positive and actually makes you feel good.

Approaches And Treatment To Panic Attacks, Phobias, Anxiety

If you've been looking for solutions to your panic attack problem, you've no doubt already run into several popular suggestions. While many of these "solutions" do have some merit, my main disappointment with them is they don't go deep enough. They don't get to the root causes of your panic attack problem, so they rarely result in dramatic, lasting improvement.

They are out there, however, and they are all heavily promoted. So I thought I should take a few moments to address twelve of the most popular ones briefly.

Reduce your intake of stimulants:

Yes, this is sound advice. Check to see if any prescription or over-the-counter medications you might be taking have stimulants in them. Even popular cold or flu remedies can contain certain stimulants that can kick off a panic attack. The same is true for diet pills, appetite suppressants, and energy drinks. And of course, if you are using cocaine, cut it out. There's no chance at all you are going to beat this problem unless you are absolutely clean and have your full wits about you.

Use Yoga, Meditation, and other:

Yoga, meditation, tai chi, massages, biofeedback, and many other relaxation techniques can help to reduce your overall anxiety level and reduce the frequency of your panic attacks. But they also don't go far enough. Meditation can be a good daily practice to help you learn how to let troubling thoughts, including scary thoughts during a panic attack, just flow right through you. Biofeedback can help you focus on controlling your breathing, reducing your heart rate, and otherwise reducing your panic symptoms during an attack. But there's usually much more to know and address to stop having panic attacks than these popular techniques can provide.

Therapy:

Therapy may sometimes be needed, and it can often be very helpful. However, therapy is expensive and can take a long time. Also, finding a good, qualified therapist can be a challenge. Some therapists are not very good at all. But if you find a good one, this can be the best option, especially if self-help resources like this one don't give you the full relief you are searching for.

Cognitive Behavior Therapy (CBT)

One of the best types of therapy to help with your panic attacks is known as Cognitive Behavior Therapy or CBT. Cognitive Behavior Therapy is successful for about 50% of panic attack suffers. It can also be very helpful for the treatment of phobias, agoraphobia, and other anxiety problems.

CBT is based on the notion that the way people think and habitually behave largely determines their emotions, including panic attacks. This therapy helps you zero in on unrealistic thoughts or detrimental behaviors that either bring on a panic attack or make them more intense or prolonged than they need to be. As you learn to gain more control over your automatic thoughts and your habitual behaviors, you can gain direct influence over your attacks and eventually extinguish them.

Many anxiety-producing thoughts feed upon each other (i.e., one negative thought begets another negative thought which begets a negative feeling, which begets additional negative thoughts, and so on...). These escalating loops can become activated before or during an attack. So once you learn to spot them, you can proactively step in and break the chain.

CBT therapists can also train you to use certain relaxation techniques, breathing techniques, and other cognitive or behavioral strategies. However, as with any type of counseling or therapy, it's crucial to find a good therapist to get results.

NOTE:

Many of the suggestions I am going to make to you in this book are based on CBT principles. Most of them can be acted upon without the need for therapy. However, if you are struggling with panic attacks after completing this book and trying my recommended plan, then I strongly encourage you to find an experienced therapist skilled in helping people eliminate panic attacks to work with you.

Medications:

Like therapy, medications can sometimes be necessary, either short-term or long-term, for more severe anxiety disorders or panic attacks. The important thing to remember about medications is that their biggest drawback is that they are primarily aimed at just the symptoms of your problem. In most cases, they do little to address the underlying causes of your panic attack problem.

If you have panic attacks that are either severe enough or frequent enough to disrupt your normal daily routines, you should probably consider getting evaluated by a health professional. While self-help strategies can eventually help you to overcome your panic attacks, it may take time for this to happen. In the meantime, while you are working on learning how to relieve your attacks in more natural ways, sometimes medication may be necessary.

Medications can be a double-edged sword. They can help, but they also can have side effects. Therefore, regardless of what medications may be recommended to you, you still have a say in the matter. Carefully assess both the advantages and disadvantages of each treatment your doctor might propose for you.

Antidepressants

Many doctors will prescribe a trial of antidepressants for someone suffering from severe panic attacks. While these medications are usually recommended for depression, they are helpful for certain types of anxiety problems as well. So if a doctor recommends antidepressants to you, it doesn't mean your doctor thinks you are depressed.

Antidepressants do not act immediately. Sometimes, they can take up to four weeks or more to begin working. Many people make the mistake of stopping these medications after just a week or two if they don't get better quickly.

Anti-Anxiety Medications

There are also anti-anxiety medications, which sometimes can help. Some of these are for short-term treatment of occasional panic attacks, while others are prescribed daily for more frequent episodes.

Remember, since medications mainly address just the symptoms and not the root causes of panic attacks, about 50% of people who eventually come off these drugs quickly go back to having more panic attacks. Some of these individuals may need to be put back on these drugs on a long term basis. Even when this is needed, it is still possible to address the root causes of your problem and eventually not require drugs at all.

Regular physical exercise:

This can help reduce both the frequency and intensity of panic attacks. However, it's also not a cure for your panic attack problem.

Alternative healing:

These can include acupuncture, chiropractic care, massage therapy, homeopathy, and many others. You can always find individuals who swear they were cured by one or more of these healing approaches. But the success rate with all of these alternative approaches is extremely low, and most do not address the root causes of your attacks.

Hypnosis:

This is an interesting option that has worked for some people but not for others. If hypnosis works for you, great, but the odds are still very low that it will. Sometimes, however, hypnosis can address some of the root causes of panic attacks by unconsciously programming you to let go of some of the irrational thoughts which might be driving your fears.

NLP:

Neurolinguistic Programming may be very good for dealing with panic attacks, provided you find a good practitioner or a good self-help resource to guide you. This is a type of rapid relief therapy that doesn't take months or years to get results. And it has been used by many to relieve and sometimes cure fears and phobias of all kinds.

EFT:

Emotional Freedom Techniques is a form of counseling that is based on various alternative medicine disciplines, such as acupuncture, energy medicine, Neurolinguistic Programming, and Thought Field Therapy. During each session, a person is guided to focus on a specific issue while rubbing or tapping on certain specific "energy points" in the body. Some people claim their panic attacks were completely cured by this technique. However, this approach is still very controversial, and many believe it does little good.

Learn deep breathing exercises:

This can actually be a great thing to learn and use if you suffer from panic attacks. However, this again does not address the root causes of your problem. It only helps you to manage and control the symptoms of your attack once it has already occurred.

Breathe Slow and Deep

This is one popular self-help strategy I do want to explore with you in more detail. Learning to use simple breathing techniques can help reduce many of your unpleasant physical sensations during a panic attack.

81

Feeling lightheaded, feeling you are unable to breathe properly, and feeling tightness in your chest is often the result of breathing very rapidly (hyperventilation) during an attack. Learning to take slow, deep breaths early on after an attack has begun can reduce these unpleasant sensations. It can also help you to shift your focus onto your breaths—breathing in and breathing out—instead of keeping your focus on all the scary thoughts racing through your mind.

How To Help Someone With Panic Attacks

It may be frightening to see your friend or loved one having a panic attack, especially if you don't know what's going on. How should you act in these situations?

There's no reason to be afraid, and it may seem like they are overreacting or even going insane. What to say or do, what not to say? Should you stay or leave them alone going through it if they say they want you to leave?

What to do if it's your best friend, a family member, or your partner? Will it last forever? Will it change your life, your friendship, your relationship? It's a lot of confusion and worry.

If you want to be a supportive friend or loved one, firstly get informed. Learn more about it what your loved one is experiencing.

The more informed you become, the better you will understand them, and the better support you'll be.

This book and many other self-help books on this topic are a great help not only for those who suffer from panic but for those who want to support someone with this problem.

You will learn what a panic attack is, why it happens and what you can do. You'll also realize that your loved one is not going crazy but is certainly going through hard times. The good news is that panic attacks are among the most treatable mental issues, and they won't last forever.

Stay calm

This will bring some sense of control to the chaotic situation, and make your friend feel safe. If you remain calm, that's a sign to them that everything is still fine, and their fear is probably irrational. By doing so, you'll be able to help the one who is suffering.

Be there, stick around

Never, ever leave a person suffering from a panic attack alone. Anxiety will only get much worse. Even if you don't know what to do, you are talking nonsense, and you see yourself that you are not helping, just stay there. Sometimes that is enough. Even if the person demands you leave, don't do it. If you have to give them some space, keep the sufferer in your sight.

Be patient

Most panic attacks reach their peak in about ten minutes. It may last from five to thirty minutes overall. This is no matter how many times the person has gone through an attack before. Every single time it's the same frightening experience. The sufferer doesn't get used to it. No one could get used to it. So, be patient. The one who is feeling the worst is the person having the attack, not you.

Remind your friend they're not crazy.

Remind them it's a panic attack.

Sometimes it may be hard to remember that what's going on is a panic attack. Although that may seem obvious, it may be incredibly helpful to remind your friend of that simple fact.

Make sure that they have enough space.

It's important to afford enough space, literally and in every other way. Hyperventilation during the attack makes the person feel that he or she needs more air. If it's too crowded, it may make the symptoms worse because the sufferer feels trapped and under more pressure.

Suggest moving to a quiet spot.

We don't suggest escaping the situation but moving to a quiet spot nearby may be a good solution. For a too stimulated mind, it's good to limit stimuli.

Help them ride out the attack.

If you stay there with your loved one during the episode, especially if you know what you're doing, this will be a precious, learning experience for them. Having a trusted person by your side while having an attack makes things far more manageable. This may make future attacks more bearable, or even prevent them happening.

Ask proper questions.

Don't bombard the panicking friend with stupid questions - obvious, pointless, or those they can't answer. He or she knows about as much as you do about why the attack is happening.

It's okay to ask the person what they need and what to change in their current environment to help.

It's also okay to ask if he or she has had any attacks before, and if they passed. This will remind your friend that it's just a temporary state, and not dangerous.

You can try to ask questions about something you know your friend is interested in, to change their focus. But if you do it too obviously, it won't work.

Help them breathe calmly and slowly.

Breathing can help with an attack, but only if you are doing it right. Breathe with your loved one. Remind him or her to breathe in through the nose and count together: one, two, three, four. Then exhale through the mouth like you are blowing up balloons and count to four again.

Help them to focus and stay present.

Don't try with things like, "look at that bird!" It won't work, your friend is not a child. Instead, remind them to focus on their breathing, and to notice things with their senses. Ask them to name five things they can see, four they can hear, three they can touch, two they can smell, and one they can taste.

Encourage getting help.

When the episode is over, help your loved one to find a professional. That should be a licensed therapist for working with panic attacks and panic disorder. It's usually a practitioner of Cognitive Behavioral Therapy or exposure therapy.

You can also find for him or her a website for help with panic - there are a lot of places online where people with this problem can get in touch and share their experiences and help each other with advice. It's easier when you know you're not the only one with this kind of challenge.

Recommend self-help books. That can be an excellent guide for solving issues. If you read self-help books about how to deal with panic, you'll be better informed, learn how to help, and know which of them to recommend to your friend. These books may be game-changers.

Besides things you should do during someone's attack, there are indeed some things you should avoid.

Don't panic yourself. If both of you are panicking, there will be no one to help. It's your job to stay calm and bring some order into the chaos. Panic attacks always end in no more than half an hour. It's not dangerous, and it won't harm your loved one, stay calm.

Don't let the denial trick you.

Many people tend say everything's okay, even if it obviously is not. Don't let that fool you. If there are symptoms of a panic attack, it's that what's going on. "Everything's fine. I don't need help. You don't need to stay with me." - that's anxiety talking.

Don't say thing like relax, don't worry or calm down. The person would like to calm down. And she or he would really like to be relaxed instead of having a panic attack. And the fact that you don't see the reason for the fear which seems totally real for them doesn't make things easier. So, he or she cannot relax, calm down or stop worrying. Otherwise, it wouldn't be a panic attack. Just don't.

Don't minimize the problem. It's the opposite of understanding and compassion. Try to understand how big and scary their monsters are. Of course, you shouldn't make them even bigger. Accept the panic attack for what it is - an attack of intense fear, a mental issue, but not harmful, and one of the most treatable — no more, no less.

Don't judge or blame. The person isn't guilty for having a health problem. They're the one who is annoyed, angry, and frightened. Take care not to have any judgment in your look or words.

Don't help to avoid the situation. When you know your friend or family member has a problem with panic, don't let him or her avoid situations. What they need to understand is that the problem is in their thoughts, not the place, location, a person. Otherwise, he or she may become very dependent on you and avoid more and more situations until the situation becomes too hard to deal with.

When it's about escaping a situation, keep in mind that escaping now leads to avoidance later. It's crucial to understand the difference, and the exact reason - the thoughts are to blame for the attack, not circumstances.

Take Control Of Your Life

The final process of ending anxiety in a decisive manner entails creating a buffer to keep it off your life. Taking your life back entails a shift from the anxiety-filled life toward more fulfilled living, with positive goal chasing behavior meant to enhance the quality of your life

You can do this by creating happy memories through leisure, creating a vision for your life, reconnecting with nature, making use of support groups like friends and family, positive thinking, and harnessing anxiety for optimal performance. Happy memories are especially useful when you are dealing with trauma and bad experiences. They give you something positive to focus on as you battle anxiety and panic attacks.

Leisure activities

Anxiety and stress are usually a result of burdens that we carry from work, family, and relationships. People with more responsibilities struggle with anxiety and stress more than those who have fewer of them because they tend to have a very transactional view of time. Any time spent doing nothing is seen as time wasted. To compensate for this, they fill every waking moment with 'productive' activities. Yet unstructured time is proven to be one of the most important times of your day because it gives you the opportunity to explore the more playful parts of your mind. The activities that you engage in during unstructured time are very relaxing. Even at work, they prevent burnout and increase overall productivity. Leisure activities give the brain some downtime, which counterbalances the hard work that occupies the majority of all other times. Good leisure activities include:

Games

Games are relaxing whether they involve intense physical activity like tennis or they entail limited physical activity like video games. But even within the world of play, you can reap a lot more rewards than just relaxing the mind. With physically intense games, you get some exercise, which is, of itself, very effective in boosting our resistance to stress. On the other hand, strategic games like chess sharpen our mental faculties and helps us improve our overall problem-solving skills. In fact, the important part of gaming is that it allows us to connect with friends. That camaraderie is a very important ingredient in the overall well-being of humans.

Running is one of the best ways to start the morning. It invigorates your body, gives you time to think, and produces stress-reducing endorphins into the body. But aside from these benefits, running can be used in a therapeutic manner to overcome anxiety and stress.

Reading

Nothing beats curling up in a comfortable chair with a good book and a warm cup of coffee as the snow falls against the window outside. A good book takes you into a whole new world and opens your mind to new possibilities. If you have some stress that you want to escape from, a good thriller or whirlwind romance can be just the thing to give you that. For the duration of reading that book, your anxiety and stress will be offset by the tension of what happens next in your current read. In the meantime, the problem is being ruminated at the back of your mind and the solution will jump at you at the most unexpected moment. Activities like reading that engage the mind facilitate background rumination, which helps to solve problems. But even more importantly, books enhance feelings of empathy and helps us relate to other people's feelings much better.

Watch television

Television, especially the news, can be a huge trigger for stress and anxiety. However, in some ways, television can be a perfect relaxation tool. Coming off of work and settling back for an evening of television and popcorn can be a perfect way to unwind. And you can get a few laughs while you are at it by watching comedy shows and dramas, which engage some of the same areas of the mind as reading a novel. You can get a little of the same high you got by watching your best shows by indulging in a re-run–one way that you can never go wrong with television.

Goof off

One type of leisure that most people do not appreciate is simply plopping down on a couch and simply doing nothing. You can nod off, go for a long walk to nowhere, visit a friend and catch up, or eat a long meal, but that is simply your time to rewind.

Create a vision for your life

A vision acts like a beacon of light pointing you toward the right direction as you navigate through life. A vision forces you to think big and then that huge ideal that you decide to pursue becomes a big motivation for you to dedicate all your energies to a particular idea. The process of creating a vision entails resolving old wounds, discovering your place in the world, and exploring one's passions.

The process of resolving old wounds entails the use of CBT and EFT to get to the root of anxiety and self-sabotage to build confidence. Old wounds are some of the greatest hindrances to commitments, even to visions and life goals. Until you have resolved old wounds that have been holding you back, you cannot go too far before sabotaging yourself, losing momentum, or otherwise slowing down. Getting to the root cause of anxiety and resolving it frees the mind from its experiential cage.

In seeking to discover your place in the world, the psych-k process of activating the superconscious part of the mind comes very handy. As you discover your place, you also try to determine what your purpose in life is. A vision based on one's life purpose will always be successful. And once you discover your purpose in life, you will receive a boost of confidence and purpose, which allows you to keep any residual anxiety at bay.

Finally, creating a vision for your life based on your passion gives you the ultimate gift in that you will always be doing something that you take great pride in. As the saying goes, when you do something you love, you will never have to work a day in your life. Doing something at which you excel is one of the best and surefire confidence builders you can find. This will also allow you to avoid anxiety that comes from workplace stress.

Nature appreciation

Spending all your time in the build environment increases anxiety, sadness, and feelings of hopelessness. The constant rubble of honking cars, motor vehicle fumes, overcrowded spaces, and limited access to the open skies in one thing that builds muscle tension, suppresses the immune system, and elevates the heart rate. Humans have spent an overwhelming part of history in nature, so our spirits are naturally built to thrive in nature as well.

In dealing with anxiety, we are naturally drawn to nature. This is because:

Nature soothes

Walking in the natural shade of tree, listening to the gurgling of water as it flows down a river, watching the water ripple in a lake, or observing the waves breaking against the land in an ocean are all very soothing activities that force the heart to slow down and take it all in. There is something in nature that just makes you want to stop and take notice. Genetically, we are programmed to get distracted and find refuge in the elements, which is why trees, water, or the night sky is likely to make you forget about your inner pain and stress for a while. If you can use your nature visitation as a therapy and try to connect with it, you will realize a place of tranquility like no other.

Nature heals

Spending a few hours in nature has been found to bring the levels of stress, fear, and anger down and increase the feelings of wonderment and peace. But even more than emotional health, nature improves our physical health as well. Moreover, you do not necessarily have to be outside to appreciate nature. You can reap the rewards by simply placing a potted plant in your house. Caring for plants is another way that we increase the connection we feel to Mother Nature and heal emotional and spiritual scars for greater state of well-being.

Restores

In a study, 95% of people who described their mood as anxious, stressed, or depressed reported an improvement to a more tranquil and balanced state after a few hours spent out in nature (Mcgonigal, 2016). Nature has been shown in numerous other studies to restore positive feelings and improve vitality and meaning for life. Children with ADHD-related anxiety reported an improvement in their ability to concentrate after being introduced to activities like bird watching, hiking, and camping. And when people spend a few nights out camping, their sense of self-reliance improves, bringing down their anxiety levels in turn.

Nature connects

Hardly will you ever go into the wilderness alone. Activities like camping, fishing, hiking, and bird watching are best enjoyed as a group. Families that spend at least one week every year camping have been shown to have a stronger bond and couples who engage in nature-related recreational activities are stronger as well. So, not only does nature make you feel more grounded and connected to Mother Earth, it also strengthens interpersonal bonds.

In fact, nature fosters stronger connections even among strangers. People who live in housing projects that incorporate green space to the design have happier, stronger, and supportive neighborly relationships. These neighborhoods also have less street crime.

Go outside in nature and spend time there.

Some studies have linked higher levels of depression and anxiety to individuals who spend a lot of their time interacting with technology within the house. The more TV and computer time you have, the greater your chances of developing anxiety become. This is caused by deprivation of nature. Interacting with other people only through screens also reduces the level of empathy a person feels as well as their willingness to help those in need. A lower level of altruism is one characteristic that is attributed to these people as well, especially when a lot of this time is spent in isolation.

Travel

Travel is a very complicated topic when it comes to anxiety. On one hand, it is one way to improve the quality of your life, overcome anxiety, and live wholesomely. On the other hand, being in a new environment can be very unsettling for some people.

94

Benefits of travel

Taking a vacation after a whole year of grueling work is one of the best ways to reward yourself. It is the ultimate way to wind down, completely disconnect from the world, and simply live in the moment. For people in the creative fields, traveling also happens to be one way of boosting creativity. Not only do you get to see new things and experience a different version of the world, you also meet new people, and observe new ways of living. This tends to open up creative pathways.

But by far the greatest benefit of travel is that you get to make so many awesome memories. Especially if you take an adventure tour, you will experience the world in a whole new way, have fun with friends or even make new ones, and expand your reserve of happy memories for the future. Finally, the prospect of annual vacations motivates you to work hard. As you work harder to be able to take a vacation, all other areas of your life benefit from the increased cash flow as well.

Dealing with travel anxiety

You cannot reap the benefits of travel without dealing with the anxiety that comes with traveling to new places and living life differently. This anxiety can even make you bail out of traveling altogether and miss out on the great benefits of travel.

Some of the ways that you can deal with travel anxiety includes doing it with friends, forming a routine or taking packaged tours to limit your choices during travel.

Support groups

Living a wholesome life depends in a huge way on the social support you get from friends and family. We are social beings and crave the connection of other people, without which anxiety levels rise and quality of life drops quite drastically. Support groups can be either therapy-based or just social groups.

The therapy-based kind is used in treating anxiety. Anyone who has ever had a panic attack or dealt with acute or chronic anxiety know that the worst thing about anxiety is that it makes one feel like they are alone in their fears. The isolation of anxiety increases the anxiety because one feels that they are 'weird' or 'abnormal' in some way. However, once you join a support group, you get to interact with people going through the same thing. This normalizes your anxiety attacks and gradually helps you to get a grasp on them.

Spend and enjoy the time with friends and family

A social support group is very important for overall well-being in life. It enables you to maintain your mental health by being there for you when you need some support. And other than acting as your support group, the time you spend with your friends and family contributes to the store of happy memories that you can summon when you want to overcome a panic attack.

Laugh a lot it's very important

Laughter is medicine for the soul and something that we all need to maintain proper spiritual and emotional health. The secret to well-being and living a great life is to pursue happy memories wherever you might find them. Let no day go by that you do not hear a joke, make one, or share one. Even if you will need to subscribe to some meme channel or watch funny videos on YouTube, ensure that you have a hearty laugh each day.

Harness Anxiety for Optimal Performance

Anxiety is a product of human evolution that helps to keep us safe from dangers –real or imagined–around us. As someone who has experienced anxiety or panic attacks, you probably know a thing or two about the power of anxiety. Anxiety powers us to overpower, outrun, and outsmart foes that could not have a hope of overpowering in our luckiest day otherwise. The body produces higher levels of adrenaline during panic attacks to power the muscles to fight a scary enemy or run away, but this power is not limited to these two evolutionary functions.

You see, we have learned to fear anxiety because it gets in the way of us being "normal" and scares the living daylights out of us. But the aim of an anxious mind is not to get in your way. It is to keep us safe from danger. The problem arises when we try to convince this part of the brain that there is no danger that requires us to get all excited. This conflict within the mind is what worsens anxiety and makes it harder to live with ourselves.

So, what would happen if you were to decide to get out of the way of your own mind instead? Could you harness the power of your anxious mind to produce terrific results in any area of your life you desire? Well, as it turns out, the answer to these questions is that yes, it is possible to harness anxiety. Instead of dealing with it as mind against mind, you can give both minds something to focus on instead. Like a work project, life vision, or any other objective. In fact, anxiety is one of the ingredients necessary to achieve the state of flow, which allows one to attain the highest level of focus and optimum productivity in a particular task.

Keeping Diary Benefits

Before looking at the benefits of the diary, first I must show you or tell you what it is. A diary is a book in which someone writes down their feelings and thoughts. It usually has a dated for every record written down.

So the first benefit of a diary is that it first helps one to keep one's thoughts very organized. Since in a diary all thoughts and feelings are poured down it is easy to know what one is thinking. This happens since these feelings and thoughts are dated every day. One can keep track of how they are behaving and thinking from these accounts. The feelings poured down in the diary act as a mirror to our mind and bodies thus letting us understand ourselves much better. This is one of the best reasons that make a diary important.

The second benefit is that it helps to improve one's writing. We say that practice makes perfect. This is the perfect saying for this benefit. Since one writes every day about their feelings and thoughts every day that makes one master their writing. That may be on one's writing style or even the mastery of language. Both of these aspects need one to practice. Since one may have no time to do that then the diary acts like compensation to that issue. So the more one writes in that diary the better they become at the end with their writing.

Another benefit is that one can be able to set whatever goals they aspire to have at the end. Since in a diary one is writing their feelings and thoughts of their day then they can set their goals in there. Goals are what someone aspires to have at the end of a certain period of time. When someone has noted their goals and aspirations in their dairy then they can easily go back. This means that one can check them as a reminder and also one can look at their progress to finally getting them in the long run.

The other benefit of a diary is that one records their ideas there and then. A diary is used for feelings and thoughts. It does not matter whether they are current or past. The recording of one's utmost feelings and thoughts make one record their ideas in the process. One gets to do this every day and that means fresh new ideas come up every time. This helps to show man's creative side. It also shows the ability of man to come up with anything during the course of the day or even the course of days.

Another thing is that it helps to relieve stress. This is one of the most important benefits of all. This is because it is greatly related to the title of this book. The diary is for keeping the thought and feelings. When one is feeling down or happy they end up writing how they feel at the end of the day. When you feel sad then you write about it all the bad feelings or the sad feeling go away. They all go to writing and they leave the person feeling free. Writing makes you feel better and very free.

Also, a diary helps to do a self-evaluation or one is able to self-reflect. This means one is able to measure oneself at the end of it all. One is able to see how much they have achieved or not achieved in the day. After a long day, one looks at the day he or she had and writes about it. One looks at the areas where one can change and the areas he or she needs appreciation. This is a way to keep one in point. It is a great way to make yourself a better person for others and for you too.

The last thing is that it increases your memory of things. When you write something it becomes easy to remember it because you think of it then you jot it down. This actually the most advisable form of remembrance this is because man has no photographic memory. The diary helps one to remember the things one has done. This a place in which one can actually refer to thus this makes it very good in terms of memory keeping. This is very important and it also helps to keep the secrets one is not willing to share and acts as a reminder.

Write a Diary without Leaving Rules

The diary is a book in which we right thought and feelings. It is usually written what someone really wants to write about. Over the years people have thought diary writing is only for teenage girls. This is such a bad misconception that should be removed. So how do we write a diary and what are the rules? Are there even rules? The answer to this question is that there are no rules to diary writing but there rules that can be followed to perfect dairy writing skills in a person or people.

The first tip is to ensure that you are honest. A diary is the most sacred and personal form of written material in someone's life. One is in a safe space when writing in a diary and one can write anything. One knows that the information put in can be kept as a secret. The innermost thoughts and dreams are what one can put in the diary. This is usually the best place to communicate with the utmost discretion. One is not afraid of their secrets being found out. So pouring their hearts out is something that should happen.

The other tip is that it should be detailed. One of the benefits of a diary is that they act as someone's memory. This means that one can refer to their events or all the things that they planned before. So the accounts of someone's diary should have a lot of information. Everything should be stated clearly with no fear. The no fear is because the secrets are very safe in that enclosed book. Every time you need to look back at something then you can and you will know what really went down. That will be curtsey of the detailed information.

Another thing is that one should check on the spelling of their writing. There is a benefit to doing this is that it helps to improve one's writing. One is forced to look at their grammar. One gets to master their language and writing altogether. This helps someone in their personal and professional life. It makes someone thrive in these two sectors of life. This tip helps one to be a great writer. It works on great practice which diary writing gives every single day. This is a very important tip to always keep in mind.

The other important tip is the date. In a diary, the dates are placed on every writing that is done. One keeps a record of what they wrote and when they wrote it. That gives an organized show to someone's feelings and thoughts. It helps one know what was done on what day and how the events took place step by step. This is very good in the referencing part of life. This helps to keep the memories in check and not jumbled. The organization of the dates make it look like a sophisticated filling system but at a personal level.

Also, there is the tip of writing something short and precise. This is major since it determines how you will write. The more you write the less you make sense. That means one loses their creativity and one starts to write fantasies or made-up things. To avoid this then one should avoid long stories. So the tip on short and precise stories that you can be able to write. If you get used to writing then you can increase the entry you put in when writing. This is done when one has mastered their language and of course their grammar.

Finally, there is no need to panic if one cannot record their events every day. It has no rules on how one is supposed to fill their diary. The schedule depends on the owner of the diary. One should be free to fill it according to their likes. That means any day and at any time. That means a lot of freedom and one is able to trust themselves infill their entries. As one fills their dairy it becomes a habit that is really fun and that makes it a daily activity that one does not want to miss doing.

These tips help you to know how to handle a diary. They also show you the importance of a diary. They help to remove all the diary misconceptions that exist. This is a great way to understand more of writing and keeping records for the future. These are the proper ways to write a diary

Techniques and Tips to Keep a Diary

The diary has been seen to be important. It acts like a memory, a friend and also a stress reliever. It helps someone to know their past events. It helps one to set goals and finally being able to monitor your progress to getting them.

The first technique is to make sure that the dairy shows who you really are. This refers to it showing your actual personality. That means making the dairy in your own personal style. That means it cannot only be written one can put up photos or a piece of item that represents what he or she did during the day. It makes someone fill confident and good. It is called customizing into what you really are into. That makes it easy and that anyone can do it since not all people like the writing thing they see as a lot of work.

The other thing is putting some basic personal information of a person on the front page of the diary. It gives like a mirror show of the owner of the diary. It helps one to know themselves and to give a description of yourself to the diary. It shows a sense of ownership. It also helps one to know the owner if it ever got lost. Some of the information may include your phone number, your best friends, your name and even the place of work, home or school too. This is also a major tip.

Also make your first entry to have labels such as the week, day, time and the place of entry. This is done as a show of trust. One writes as if he or she is talking to someone. This may be writing done as if one is doing it for a friend. The diary is like a friend but a silent one. It helps you through hard patches by letting you talk about it. They listen and do not say anything back. This small fact makes it a trustworthy way of keeping all your secrets from other people's ears.

Another tip is to not be afraid of filling your diary and you may also name it. The diary is supposed to be a friend but a silent one. It should be that person you talk to when you trust no one. So giving the diary a name is a good idea. The name is a good starter for this new friendship. The name gives you a good reference as you talk. One feels as if they are in communication with a real person. It makes it seem less boring when the diary is not given a name to go by.

The other is starting again after one had a break. The diary has no schedule and one can fill the diary as they please. So one can take a break and return. Filling it every day is not a must or you have to do is fill it when you feel the need to. Although once you get the hang of filling the diary, it becomes a regular habit which is really fun. The choice, in this case, will always be on the owner's shoulders. The break is needed since it works like a regular and normal human friend.

Also, the other tip is going through the old entries and compare the difference. This is to work as a reference.

The diary entries are to be treated like letters and should be treasured for the coming future. Look at the past and see where you came from and where you are headed to. This is not meant to make you hate yourself but it is meant to show you your progress. Progress is what makes us all. It helps one appreciate themselves and see what you really are worth. This makes one be great at what they do.

The last thing is that you should hide your diary safely. One does have to do this for the safety of your secrets. The dairy is where someone writes their inner thoughts, feelings, and aspirations. Most people do not want others to find out. It is usually their safe space and it should be only for your eyes. Some people make safes for them or even others lock it in place that is away from people's sight. They are mostly put in someone's bedroom since it is someone's personal space. This is the biggest tip to maintaining your secrets and thoughts.

Increasing Your Self-Awareness

You may have noticed that there is a theme that is going on when it comes to increasing your own emotional intelligence. This theme is all about helping you to recognize what is going on in your own life, such as your emotional triggers, so you can be ready when they come up in day-to-day life.

Introspection is a skill that those with high emotional intelligence will naturally possess. Not everyone will be born with this skill, but it is something that you can work on over time. One of the first questions that you should ask yourself is "How do I know that I need to be more self-aware?" Have you made mistakes, let your emotions taken over, or done and said things that you later regret? If you have, then that means it is time to work on your self-awareness.

It is important not to focus on the negatives during this exercise. Everyone makes mistakes or does things they regret but recognizing that you have done these and that you need to work on them is the first step forward. Focus on where you want to go, not where you have been. Let's take a look at some of the steps you can take to raise your own self-awareness.

Developing self-awareness

To start, you need to take some time to be by yourself. Maybe set aside half an hour or so for this and bring along a pen and paper; sometimes it helps if you are able to write down all of your thoughts and feelings. When you are ready, it is time to take a look at some of your patterns of action and thought. Some of the things that you can consider asking yourself during this period include:

• Why do you enjoy the entertainment that you choose?

• What features attracted you to the people that you love?

• What makes you avoid doing certain things?

• What are some of your values and what do you want out of life? What do you not want?

• What are your thoughts on lying? Are your morals and character clear?

- Are you a generally happy person or do you act tired and stressed all of the time? How might these emotions be interpreted by others?

- How do you think others perceive you?

Often your attitudes about a situation are going to be based on your expectations, which are often exaggerated by your emotions or are otherwise unrealistic. Having an attitude that is positive is going to help you out so much more compared to a negative attitude because it will help you to gain strength to deal with any situation you encounter.

An example of holding onto negative attitudes occurs when it comes to your own potential. Just saying the words "I can't do that" will limit your potential and once you say the words, you never will accomplish your goals. You would be surprised at what you are capable of doing if you just put your mind to it. If you switch your thinking around to "I can do that!" you will see that you can push yourself so much further than you originally believed.

Some people who are working on their own self-awareness will choose to keep some form of a journal. They will keep track of their feelings, their day, or any other information that they deem important. After some time, take a look through the journal again and you may find out that some attitudes or events that you have will lead to others. You can also see that many of the things that you overreacted to in the past are not that important now, and it may lead you to reexamine some of the ways you react to similar events in the future.

And finally, you need to make sure to learn how to acknowledge your actions. This one can be hard, especially if you are not all that proud of the actions that you were taking. But you have to acknowledge your actions, even when they are not bringing you the results that you want. When you start to notice that an action isn't making you feel good or it is not getting you to a place you want to be, you may start to react in a different way.

Self-awareness through the perceptions of others

The second part of this process is to learn how to find your own self-awareness based on the way that others perceive you. If possible, take some time to ask your family and friends how they perceive you. In most cases, you will probably need to spend time asking yourself questions though, since most of the time those closest to you will have a hard time answering these questions. Some of the questions that you should be asking yourself concerning your character and identity include:

- Do I spend time smiling or mostly frowning?
- Is my handshake firm when I meet someone new?
- Do I have trouble making eye contact with people?
- What are some characteristics of my walk?
- Do I stand up tall or do I slouch?

Once you have been able to talk to a few people about their perception of you (but make sure you are working with people who are going to give you honest opinions), and you have your own answers, it is time to analyze the feedback. With this feedback, you will be able to go about the process of addressing the answers you don't like. For example, you can work on standing up taller or looking people in the eyes when they talk to you. You can work on smiling instead of frowning. Each person will have different points to work on and you will be able to personalize your plan to meet what perceptions you want to change.

Staying aware

Finally, it is important that once you have received your feedback and made some of the small changes, you learn how to stay aware of how you are thinking and acting. This is going to help you in so many ways including being aware of your perceptions and the emotions that otherwise would take over your life.

The first thing that you should work on is to gauge your progress during the day. You can take just five minutes at some point during the day to see if you are reaching your goals. Did you try smiling more or do you need to do a bit better? Did you stand up tall when you walked? You may have a few different characteristics that you want to work on, but just focus on one at a time. Often one will tie into the others and you will automatically start doing them all in response.

And finally, you need to develop your own attitude of mindfulness so that you are aware that there are things that go on beyond your private little world. Many of the problems that arise with our emotions occur because we have learned how to be on autopilot and we just react when things don't go the way that we would like. When we learn that not everything is important, that some people react because they had a bad day and not because of anything to do with us, we can gain a better control of our own emotions.

Conclusion

Panic attacks & anxiety are very awful ailments that even the healthiest human being on the Earth can get them at some point in his/her life. However, it is curable and I have now shown you my methods eliminating them.

There is no magic trick to get rid of panic attacks and anxiety in one day, but rather you need to work for it.

You have two ways of treating these ailments. It can either be through medicines or naturally. According to my journey, I have taught you how to do it naturally without any medicine.

My method started from the identification of the current state of personal self, by observing personal self and finding out the root causes of panic attacks and anxiety. Once we found those reasons the next step was to find out the sources of those causes. So, it is like digging deep until you find a concrete reason that you need to tackle down. For example, in my case the concrete reason was too much stress.

Then, the next step was to take down each of those sources one by one. This way we also make sure that we are able to get back to our healthy state surely and also it would be easier to tackle down each source for good. If you try to take down all the sources at the same time, it might be difficult to succeed. The reason behind this is that by doing so many things at the same time it is difficult to manage and achieve, but by doing one thing at a time there would be a higher chance of achieving success in it because you can concentrate on it.

And when you have succeeded in taking down your panic attacks and anxiety through the methods that I have taught, you would notice that there was no need for medicines. However, no matter the situation you are in, you should always start first by meeting psychologist. It helps by talking to a professional.

But always remember that you have two options; either through medicines or natural way.

Now, you have very valuable information in your hand. You have learned many valuable lessons which will help you beat panic attacks and anxiety for good. Not only that, but you have also gotten methods of recognizing stress and how to prevent it before it is starts. Through this you are able to prevent panic attacks and anxiety before they even happen.

If you are suffering from panic attacks and anxiety, then it's time for you to beat those ailments. If you have read this book just to get more information about panic attack and anxiety for sake of interest or because you want to help someone that is close to you who's having panic attacks and anxiety, then you have done more than enough.

Thank you for reading this eBook and I really hope that it has been useful.

One last thing I want to say to you if you have decided to start beating your panic attacks and anxiety in natural ways then,

I BELIEVE IN YOU TO GET RID OF PANIC ATTACKS AND ANXIETY FOR GOOD!

ANXIETY THERAPY

Introduction

Depression is a severe common psychological disorder that has an emotional impact on how you think, how you feel, and how you act. In this regard, depression results in an emotional state of sadness and continuous disinterest with activities that someone once liked. Fortunately, this disorder is treatable despite the detrimental effects that it possesses on an individual. In the current society, depression has become one of the significant health concerns that have necessitated governments and institutions to engage in an educative undertaking to inform the public on the prevalence of depressive symptoms among youths and the general populace within any community. It is quite certain that you as an individual, in one way or another, have heard or read the information that pertains to depression, or better still through mainstream media outlets understood discussions that were based on despair and its impact on the community as a whole.

Depressive indications can vary from trivial to severe states that involve having or possessing thoughts about death or suicide, concentration difficulty, loss of productive energy or increased exhaustion, continuous feelings of sadness, trouble sleeping, and feeling worthless among many other indicators. Even though it is apparent that in one instance one can possess some of the symptoms identified above, you should note that for a diagnosis of depression to be passed then these symptoms should last for at least two weeks. This is because, some of the warning signs associated with depression are sometimes encountered or experienced daily; thus, one can rush into the conclusion that they are depressed. Unfortunately, this might not be the case, since for such symptoms to be regarded as signs of depression, they have to last for at least two weeks. As a result, researchers have stated that depression is very much different from sadness or mourning. This is because it is a regular occurrence for feelings of sadness and withdrawal from daily lifestyle to develop as a response to the situation: being sad does not signal that you are depressed. Since such occurrences share similar features to depression, they possess different characteristics and qualities.

Anxiety is very different from depression since it entails fear that is characterized by behavioral disturbances. From this perspective, you can discern that anxiety is an intense, excessive, and continuous fear and worry about daily experiences or situations that are characterized by fast breathing, increased heart rate, and sweating to mention a few. Although there are common causes of anxiety that do not have a significant impact or effect on your life. Some of these common causes include public speaking, taking a test or exam, or going for an interview. Anxiety only becomes problematic when possessing anxious feelings to become consistent and persistent that they start to interfere with your regular life. This brings us to the topic of anxiety disorders, a group of mental illnesses that affect you from carrying on with your daily life. The good news about having such kind of complications is that it is treatable just like depression is.

Having that anxiety disorder can be treated, one recommended approach for managing such a condition that you are likely to encounter is therapy for anxiety disorders or mentioned as anxiety therapy. Anxiety therapy comes out as the best option for treating anxiety when compared to medication.

Identifying Problem and Negative Thoughts Patterns

Social anxiety comes with harmful and destructive thoughts. You need to be observant so that you do not hurt yourself in the process. The negative thinking is likely to rob you of the confidence that you have and feel that you cannot stand going before people. The thoughts instill fear in you, and you end up avoiding social gatherings. When you subject your opinions to negative thinking always, it will result in negative emotions. It can end up making you feel bad and can even lead to depression. The thoughts that you have will determine your mood for your entire day. Positive thinking will make you happy, and you will have a good feeling. Finding a way to suppress negative thoughts will be of importance to you. Replace them with positive ones so that they will not torment you. Some of the negative thoughts that come along with social anxiety are;

Thinking That People as bad

When you are in a social setting, each person tends to be busy with their issues. You can meet a calm person and begin a friendship if you can build a good rapport. When you have social anxiety, you are likely to avoid people and think that people do not care about you. You may feel that you don't see your importance being there while as you are the one who is avoiding them. When you find yourself in such a situation in a social setting, its time you know that you have to handle your social anxiety. That will make you feel like the people around you do not like you and hate you for no reason.

Unnecessary Worry

It is obvious to have unnecessary worry when you have social anxiety. Even when you are on time, you are always worried that you will get late. You will portray a bad image for getting there late. When in a family setting, you are worried that your partner will scold you for lateness. You do things in a hurry so that you do not get late even when you have enough time to go to your thoughts. When you have someone else to accompany you, you will make them do things in a rush. You think like they are consuming all the time and they will be your reason for being late. You will even, at times, threaten to leave them if they don't do things quicker than they are already doing.

When you are needed to make a presentation, you get worried about whether the audience is going to like it or not. You are not sure whether there is someone else who will do better than you. The worry will make you start thinking that your boss will not like what you have even before they make their remarks. You believe that you have nothing exciting to say. The worry will make you lose strength, and any change you feel makes you think that you are not ready. When you start experiencing such concern, you need to know that you have social anxiety. You require to have an approach that is appropriate to handle your social stress so that it will not escalate into something worse.

Judging Yourself

Judging yourself is the worst thing you will ever go, and that will make you fear. Deciding whether you will find pleas people or not will make you have much social anxiety. You will be nervous when you start thinking about how people are thinking about your physical appearance. Judging how you other people will view you will make your self-esteem go down. The people you are worried about will think you do not look outstanding may not have an interest in how you look but what you have to deliver. At times, people do not pay attention to the minor details that are making you judge yourself unnecessarily.

Criticism

Anytime you know that you will intermingle with people, you fear they will criticize you. You do not even have a valid reason why they will criticize you, but you think it is not wise for you to join them. It is a negative thought, and you need to stop thinking in that direction. No one is going to critic you for no reason, and that should not be considered close to you. You will fear to go to social gatherings, and you will deny yourself an opportunity to learn from your fellow partners. Fearing criticism will make you be an introvert, and this will make you mean that you will miss much when you choose to stay indoors. When you say something, and you get someone to challenge you, it will help you be more creative. Criticism is not evil even though that people with social anxiety do not like a situation where they are subject to critics. They will avoid such situations at all cost for fear of humiliation.

Negative thoughts will only escalate worry as well as fear in you. For you to avoid negative thoughts, you can practice cognitive-behavioral therapy. That will replace your negative thoughts with those that are accurate as well as encouraging. Though it will take quite some time to replace the negative thoughts, practicing healthy thinking daily will make that natural to you. If you have social anxiety and you feel that all the approaches you use are not helpful, seek the help of a therapist. Positive thinking will help you in coping with social anxiety. When you notice that you have negative thoughts disturbing you, you should try to drop that with immediate effect. Filter the bad and focus on the good. To change how you are thinking, the first thing you need to do is try and understand how your thinking pattern is at the moment. Do not view yourself as failure always because that will never change your thinking patterns. When you avoid negative thoughts, you will be in an excellent position to fight social anxiety.

Prejudgment

Although it is wise to think about the future, the art of judging tends to be detrimental. In other words, the aspect of prejudging situations tends to be worse, especially when the opposite of the expectations is meant. In most cases, social anxiety disorder tends to cause people to decide the results of a particular situation. It is worth noting that prejudgment is done in regards to the history or rather a forecast of what might happen in the future.

In most cases, the people who are involved in this practice are always negative. Thus, they will think evil of someone and need up piling unnecessary pressure on someone. There are cases where the prejudgment causes one to overthink rather than spend quality time improving on their lives. In other words, prejudgment may force one to change all her aspects in an attempt of meeting the expectations of the peers. The peers will, in most cases, demand or look for everyday things. However, there are cases where the prejudgment predicts a near future that is yet to be accomplished. The aspect causes one to fear as they loom for an alternative as well as ways of meeting the expectations. However, when the expectations aren't satisfied, the anxiety of what the society will say pile up, and one may quickly lose the focus.

Blame Transfer

When a society or the peers piles up unnecessary pressure on someone, the chances of missing the mark is quite easy. In other words, one quickly loses focus and misses the point. As a means of evading the shame or rather the punishment, the victims, in most cases, transfer the blame. For instance, if it issues to deal with academics, the victim may start claiming that time wasn't enough to deliberate on all issues. Others may associate their failures with the climatic changes or the lack of favorable conditions for working. There are cases where the victims tend to be genuine and claim diseases as the cause of their failure. However, the art of transferring blames from one point to another tends to be detrimental and shows signs of being irresponsible.

Procrastination

One of the significant effects of social anxiety is that is causes one to fail in deliberating on duties and transfer them to a later day. In other words, procrastination becomes the order of the day. However, it is worth noting that with procrastination, the expectations are never met. The fear, as well as the sensation of being anxious sets in. In other words, the victim starts feeling as if they are a failure in the collective and loses focus. More time is wasted as they try to recollect themselves up. More fear sets in and the victim may end up being restless. Improper management of time is the primary cause of procrastination. In other words, the lack of planning causes individuals to keep working over the same issues and forget about others. For instance, scholars may spend more time with the subjects they like and forget about the others. In other words, they may end up forgetting that all the items will be examined in the long run. The sensations bring more fear and restless.

In most cases, the realization that all the aspects will be tested in the long run causes most of the scholars to be anxious about the result. In most cases, the tensing moment tends to escalate when there is no time left to deliberate on all issues. The fear of failure then worsens the situation. In most cases, when the scholars realize that they haven't done all that is supposed to be done, the feeling of loss of hope and expectations of failure sets in. They start figuring about the failure they are about to experience. In other words, they start thinking of what society expects from them. The feeling of anxiety sets in, and they may not be able to deliberate on issues effectively.

Social anxiety may affect the way people lead their lives. In other words, the perception or rather the sensations that people have over someone tend to change the way one relates to society. For instance, if society expects excellence in terms of academics from you, you have to work hard and meet all their expectations. In such cases, there is a sensation of fear or rather the feeling of anxiety that sets in. One starts to fear what society will judge their actions or results.

In most cases, the victim becomes restless and quickly loses focus over issues at hand. They may start desiring to meet the expectations of their peers as well as the rest of society and in the long run, lose their purpose. The aspect creates some sense of irresponsibility that acts as a significant cause of failure and total loss when one is having extreme anxiety over anything.

Our thoughts are interconnected with our feelings and behaviors. The way we think affects both how we feel and act. The first step toward recovering from negativity is identifying various negative thinking patterns. When you take note of your negative thoughts, you get a better understanding of your mind and emotions and are in a much better position to develop positive thoughts.

Some types of negative thoughts include, I'm so stupid, I'm so foolish, and, I'm unlucky.

If you find it difficult to be introspective and admit to your negative thoughts, you should ask a trusted friend or family member to keep track of your negative ways of thought.

Find Out the Causes of Your Negative Thought Patterns

The next challenge is to identify the sources of your negative thoughts. For instance, if one of your negative thoughts is, I'm ugly, no one likes me! try to understand the action or event that triggered this thought. Being good at identifying the causes of our negative thoughts calls us to be introspective. Maybe the source of your negative thought is your childhood abuse. If a close family member told you that you are not beautiful, you might have taken it to heart, and have been since looking for evidence to support your flawed belief. A member of the opposite sex might look at you with a frown – for other reasons of course – but you will still deduct from their facial expression that they find you ugly.

Highlight Unhelpful Thought Patterns

It is one thing having negative thought patterns, and it is another having unhelpful thought patterns. These are also known as core beliefs. The unhelpful thought patterns are ingrained into a person's psyche. Unhelpful thought patterns tend to be divorced from reality. For instance, if you have been telling yourself, "I'm stupid," for long enough, it will cease being just a negative thought and graduate into a core belief. This will lead you to automatically shunning opportunities and people that you consider too smart for you.

List down the Consequences of Your Negative Thoughts

To be more involved in actively changing your negative thought patterns, you have to identify the consequences that you suffer. For instance, if your negative thought, I'm foolish causes you to detach yourself from your peers or stops you from going for the opportunities that you deserve, take note of these consequences so that you may increase your resolve to change your situation. At one point, you will have had enough and decide that you want to change. You may also list down past negative experiences and consequences that occurred as a result of negative thinking patterns.

Keep a Record of Your Thoughts

Using a worksheet, track the number of negative thoughts that you experience on a daily or weekly basis. Also, note down the ideas that support a thought and the ideas that do not support a thought. For instance, if one of your negative thoughts is, I'm a loser, ideas that do not support this negative thought include, "I'm a great person", "I have a sharp mind", and "I don't need everyone to like me!" Try to determine the days during which you experience low cases of negative thought patterns and the days when the negativity shoots through the roof.

Avoid Negative Language

Create a list of negative words that you use often. For instance, "can't" and "won't", and make a conscious decision of using more balanced words like "sometimes" or "most of the time". When you have a negative way of thinking, it affects even the language you use. But you must make a conscious effort to alter this situation. By developing a language that promotes positivity, you will be sending a message to your brain to challenge its negative thinking patterns.

Explore the Connection between Your Emotions and Negative Thoughts

Whenever you experience a negative emotion, start by questioning the thought behind it. For instance, if you get anxious or depressed, go back to the thought that you just had. You will find that the thought was depressive in nature. For instance, you might have wondered why you have taken so long to achieve success or why you haven't settled, or you might have just thought that you're not good enough. Always monitor your thoughts and take notice of the negative thoughts. When you catch a negative thought early enough, it is easy to amend it. For example, instead of thinking, I'm not good enough by means of a mantra, you want to think, I'm a great person!

Choose Positive Explanations

No matter how your actions appear conventionally terrible, you can always rationalize them. For instance, if you had a child while you're still young, instead of looking at it as throwing your dreams away, look at it as bringing something new into the world. The same case applies to your thoughts. On the occasions that you experience negative thoughts, you want to find a positive or realistic explanation.

List down the Things That You're Grateful For

When you are battling negative thoughts, it is quite easy to overlook the many positive things about your life. To shift your mindset from negativity into positivity, you have to list down the things that you are grateful for. Some of the things that you ought to be grateful for include family, lovers, pets, and home. Whenever you fall short of your expectations, think about what you already have, and close the door to negative thinking patterns.

Practice Mindfulness

Instead of getting lost in the negative thoughts roaring in your mind, learn to shift your focus to the present. Pay direct attention to the things that you are doing at that moment, such as eating, drinking, and other daily activities.

Seek Guidance and Support

Don't bury yourself in negative thinking patterns. If you have tried in vain to get rid of your unhelpful thoughts, don't feel shy to reach out to an authority for help. They understand your problem probably more than you ever will. Get close to people too. You'd be amazed at the number of kind-hearted people out there ready to help you if you choose to want their help.

Describe Automatic Thoughts and Intrusive Thoughts

What are Automatic and Intrusive Thoughts

CBT is based on the premise that it isn't the situation or circumstances that cause the condition, but the meaning assigned to these situations that lead us to experience depression or anxiety. The way we interpret a particular situation is what makes us slip into a negative state of mind. Often, the ideas that we hold about events or situations are impractical or blown out of proportion.

When these misleading notions are not challenged, they continue to grow stronger and lead to even more negativity. We assume it as our reality, which blocks us from perceiving things as they are and leading a fulfilling life. There is a tendency to overlook or ignore things that do not match our negative perception of events and situations. We continue to let these thoughts grow unhindered.

For instance, a person suffering from depression will think that he/she just can't go to the office today because nothing's going to be positive. Their thoughts operate from a sense of hopelessness. They end up believing what they think is true. So according to the person, nothing positive is bound to happen at work today, which means with their negative thought pattern there's absolutely no opportunity of knowing if this feeling is right or wrong. The person doesn't give himself/herself a chance to ascertain the veracity of their claims. Their thinking itself leads to the negative or unpleasant experience.

In the above example, the person stays at home and doesn't go to work. Thus he/she doesn't know whether their negative prediction had any clear basis. Such individuals sit at home thinking that they are an absolute failure and that they've let people down. They become angry with themselves and think about how incompetent and useless they are. This leads to the person feeling even worse than earlier, which results in more difficulty while attending office the following day. This causes a downward thinking, behavior and feeling spiral or a vicious circle that leads to several problems.

Where Do The Thoughts Originate?

According to the founder of CBT Aron Beck, the thoughts can be traced back to our childhood, when they become relatively rigid and involuntary. For instance, a child who may not have got enough attention and affection from the family but was encouraged to perform well academically may grow up with the notion that people have to be a success or do well every time. Such individuals will start believing that if they are not successful, people won't accept them. This may lead to the person putting excessive pressure on himself and slipping into depression if he fails to meet their own standards for success.

They may not experience the desired success due to something that's beyond their realm of control, which triggers the negative or dysfunctional thought. The person may believe that he/she isn't good enough or is a total failure. This will lead them to think they won't be accepted by others, and hence withdraw socially.

Cognitive behavioral therapy helps people to gain awareness of the fact that their mind is processing thoughts in a more skewed manner. It assists them in stepping out of their involuntary thought pattern and challenges these unfounded thoughts.

In the above instance, it challenges the person to assess her real-life instances for determining whether her thoughts are in congruence with reality. If something that has happened in their past or to someone else has indeed matched their perspective about the situation.

This helps them gain a greater realistic perspective, and they may end up gaining an opportunity to test the perspectives of other people by revealing their situation to close friends and family members.

There's no denying that negative things happen. However, when we are in a tough state of mind, our perspective and interpretations operate from a more biased plane. Thus we magnify the challenge we face. CBT assists people in modifying these skewed interpretations and helps them see things from a more balanced perspective.

CBT for Intrusive OCD Thoughts

Cognitive behavioral therapy points out that OCD or Obsessive Compulsive Disorder is when people misread intrusive thoughts or compelling urges as indications that harm will occur and they are directly responsible for their actions.

When it comes to treating OCD or intrusive thoughts through CBT, it helps individuals understand that their intrusive or disturbing obsessive thoughts are nothing but a result of anxiety than any real danger. OCD patients are gradually made to realize that they won't be affected or in danger if they don't give in to these thoughts.

People with OCD are desperately trying to avoid harm. Their solutions invariably end up becoming part of the issue. For instance, if you keep thinking about neutralizing your thoughts about stabbing someone, it only ends up increasing these intrusive thoughts.

The real issues, therefore, aren't these intrusive thoughts but the meaning assigned to them by an individual suffering from OCD. For example, you may experience a huge urge to act upon your intrusive thoughts or that you shouldn't have these thoughts in the first place. This places a huge level of threat, anxiety, and responsibility on you. In the above example, you'll stop meeting the person alone or stop stocking your kitchen with knives. You've succumbed to the fear. The fear is still alive, and further stops you from thinking that your fear is nothing but a skewed thought.

One of the most important aspects of using CBT to treat OCD or intrusive thoughts is that the therapist only functions as a facilitator and that it has to be practiced on your own.

Different therapists focus on different cognitive and behavioral attributes of OCD or intrusive thoughts. A cognitive focused approach will help you assess your thought patterns more keenly. For instance, you have thoughts about killing someone, which makes you feel that are a bad person for having these thoughts and you could act upon them. Your therapist will work with you to seek a different understanding of these distorted thoughts and give you an alternate technique for reacting to them.

If it's a more behavioral focused approach, it could be focused on educating yourself about how anxiety is felt by the body. It is about facing your fears and gradually taking on, and increasing the very activities you fear. For instance, if you suffer from social anxiety, your therapist will slowly get you to come out of your shell and participate in interactions on a smaller scale.

Where OCD or intrusive thoughts are concerned, the end goal of CBT is to change the brain's thought process or structure. Even if this sounds like a Herculean task, it isn't. Let's consider an example.

Let's assume you have lived in the United States of America all your life, and are used to a right-hand drive. There was no hassle of changing gears. Suddenly, you have to move to the United Kingdom, which is a left-hand drive. How will you manage?

To learn to drive left-handed, you have to unlearn right-handed driving. What makes the entire pursuit tough is that it has become a subconscious or almost involuntary process. If you've never driven left-handed, you'll initially have trouble getting used to sides, looking in the wrong direction and stepping out.

However, once you change or alter your actions and gradually get used to driving left-handed, you will learn to drive in the new direction. It comes with exposure, practice, and repetition. Repeated left handed driving experiences help you navigate corners, look in the right direction and step out with confidence. You practice this repeatedly until you've altered your brain structure.

Similarly, CBT seeks to question the veracity of your intrusive thoughts by consistent action, thus leading to a change in thought patterns. It transforms unrealistic and impractical intrusive thoughts into more real and evidence focused patterns. CBT will also help you restructure your behavior about avoiding certain things that lead to intrusive thoughts. For instance, if you experience repetitive thoughts about wanting to stab someone, you overcome avoiding holding knives or being alone with the person. Over a period of time, repeated new experiences help your brain learn to control anxiety experienced as a result of these irrational thoughts.

Setting Your Goal and Getting Started

Why Set Goals?

Goal setting is a fantastic form of self-motivation. When you set goals, you give yourself something to strive for. You have something you know you want and you are able to identify that in order to have a clear idea of what your actions are for. These goals can be anything, from getting a new job to learning a skill or meeting new people. Literally, anything you would like to achieve in life can be made into a goal. Just because anything can be made into a goal does not mean that there are no guidelines, however. By following some rules, and guidelines when setting your goals, you will learn to come up with goals that will be beneficial for you and help you change your behavior or life for the better.

Ultimately, your goal should offer you some sort of benefit, whether

Bad Goals

Before getting into what rules there are to rule-setting, let's first analyze what makes a goal bad. There are three types of goals you should seek to avoid, as they are not conducive to a healthy mindset, nor are they effective for the right reasons. These goals are goals seeking to be in certain emotional states, goals that focus on the past, or goals that are rooted in negativity. Each of these types of goals is poorly formed or unproductive for various reasons.

Emotional States

Oftentimes, when people are setting goals for therapy, they think, "I want to feel happy in my own body and mind." At face value, this is a fine goal, but in reality, it is deeply rooted in feelings. However, feelings are constantly changing and fluctuating. This means that your goal may be achieved some of the time, but no one is every happy with themselves all of the time. You cannot help that sometimes; you will be disappointed or angry in yourself for something you did or a way you behaved. Because of the instability of emotions, they should be avoided as goals.

Focus on the past

People frequently also decide to set their goals as, "I want to get back to my old self," especially if their symptoms they are hoping to fix came up later in life. It is not unusual to miss the person you used to be but remember, that person is in the past. That person you used to do not go through the hard times you are hoping to get yourself out of, nor did that person have the knowledge you do now. CBT seeks to focus on the present and fix your mental health issues through actions, not by seeking out the past. The past can never be made present again, and you should never try to root your goals in returning to a past relationship, a past personality, or past feelings. You will always fail.

Negative or avoidant goals

Just as affirmations have to be kept positive in order to be effective, so too do goals. While the goal of, "I want to avoid feeling depressed," might sound like a reasonable goal, all this is doing is making you hyper-focused on avoiding the feelings of depression. By focusing on avoiding rather than on fixing the distressing symptoms, you are running from your problem. You also set yourself up for failure, because any time you fail and feel depressed, you will feel that depression compound onto itself as you collect another piece of evidence that you are as worthless and helpless as you thought you were. Ultimately, it is best to avoid setting goals with a focus on negativity or avoidance and instead focus on goals that are active instead.

SMART Goals

Now that you understand what not to do with your goals, it is time to learn what good goals consist of. It helps to remember that SMART goals are the most effective goals, with SMART being an acronym for specific, measurable, attainable, relevant, and timely. If you remember this acronym, you will be able to make your goals work for you.

Specific

When setting your goal, you want to be as specific with what you wish to attain as possible. The more specific you are, the clearer the picture you paint in your mind of what you want to achieve. There is a huge difference between saying you want to paint your room blue instead of specifying that you specifically want a light cerulean color, and likewise, there is a difference between saying you want to manage feelings of anger and angry outbursts, and stating that you want to reduce your outbursts over the course of the month. You went from a somewhat specific goal to one that gave an exact picture of what it will be.

Measurable

Just as more specific goals are desirable, having goals that are easily measurable is also crucial to set a good, productive goal. You need to be able to quantify what success looks like so you know exactly when you reach it, whether that is stating that you will write a certain amount of words a day, or save a certain amount of money. In the example of wanting to reduce anger outbursts, you could specify that you want to reduce the total number of times you react in anger by 40%. This goal now has a quantifiable definition of success.

Attainable

Your goal needs to be something you can actually reasonably complete. The easiest way to do this is to make sure your goal can easily be broken down into smaller goals to keep you motivated and moving forward. Every time you meet a goal, you feel encouraged, which keeps you moving forward, striving to complete more of your goals. This positive feedback loop reinforces the idea of meeting your goals, motivating you to start in the first place once your body and mind realize that doing so can be both beneficial and enjoyable. For example, if you set a goal of reducing angry outbursts, specifying smaller goals may make it more realistic for you to complete. You could say that you want to make it a point to have one less angry outburst than you did the day before every day. This gives you small milestone goals that will help keep you on track to attaining the whole goal.

Realistic

By making sure your goal is realistic, you avoid setting yourself up for failure. A realistic goal for one person is not going to be the same as a realistic goal for another; a fit, experienced mountain climber may be able to set and achieve a goal of climbing a huge mountain with a month to prepare, but the vast majority of people who do not mountain climb on a regular basis would likely find themselves falling out. Likewise, it can be realistic for one person to go running every day, but someone paralyzed from the neck down will never be able to attain it. Make sure your goal is reasonable and realistic to your specific situation. If you want to alleviate your anger issues and stop having angry outbursts, you have to set a realistic goal that recognizes that the process of changing your habits and mindsets.

Timed

Defining how long your goal will take gives you a clear goal with an end in sight. You give yourself a time to complete the goal by, and anything beyond that is deemed a failure. Keep in mind that you should give yourself a reasonable amount of time to complete your goal. Be realistic about your timeline and make sure it has at least some leeway for you to complete it while still giving yourself time as a motivator to work toward it. For example, if you want to reduce your angry outbursts, you decide on one month for the timeline to begin to see a reduction of 30%.

Examples of Goals

With an understanding of what a goal needs to be SMART, you will be ready to set goals that are beneficial to your mental wellbeing. Here are a few examples of goals.

Understanding Anxiety and Anxious Mind

If you picked up a copy of this book, it is most likely because you, or someone you love, is dealing with anxiety. You may know some of the symptoms, you may even have a diagnosis, but what you may not know is exactly what an anxious mind is and why it occurs.

Anxiety can strike anyone at any time, and while there are some risk factors involved, they don't always tell us who will be affected by this. Every year over 18% of the population will suffer from some form of an anxiety disorder, and yet only around 36% of those individuals will ever seek treatment or help. This leaves a large portion of the population suffering needlessly in silence, and feeling as if they are doomed by this disease.

Just like with most disorders, anxiety is highly treatable so long as the person who has it seeks out that help. But the problem with anxiety is that, oftentimes, it makes us too anxious to reach out to anyone, and so we end up in a cycle of fear.

One of the best ways to break this cycle is to start with baby steps, building ourselves up until we can overcome the anxiety long enough to ask for help. But how do we begin? And what do those baby steps look like?

Picking up this book was step one, and just by doing that, you are already in the process of overcoming your anxiety. It may not feel like anything has changed or that you have done anything dramatic, but you already have. So, let's dive straight in and look at what exactly anxiety is.

What is Anxiety?

Anxiety isn't necessarily a bad thing and is a very common and natural response to stressful situations. Maybe it's your first day of class, or you have an upcoming job interview or are going on the first day of work—all of these situations will make us feel anxious. This is our brain warning and preparing us for what is to come, and it typically benefits us by getting us ready to face a new situation, and it will subside as soon as the new experience is over.

But what happens when that anxiety prevents us from doing something new or it refuses to go away?

When we have a persistent feeling of being anxious, or when that anxiety interferes with our day to day life, then it goes beyond just a natural, normal occurrence. This is when someone will typically be diagnosed with having an anxiety disorder, and this is a common diagnosis that many people face.

You may hear people use the word "anxious" very frivolously, when in fact they mean to say that they are worried about something. "I'm so anxious about that upcoming test" would more appropriately be worded as "I'm so worried about that upcoming test." Making a distinction between worry and anxiety is extremely important, as one is normal, and one can be a serious problem.

The differences between worry and anxiety are very distinct and knowing which term to use in what situation can help you better identify if what you are feeling is normal or not. So, what should you look for to determine what exactly you are feeling?

- Being worried typically makes us feel mildly uncomfortable, whereas anxiety will make us extremely uncomfortable.

- Worry generally leads to mental problem solving, whereas anxiety causes a spiral with no solution.

- Worry is often based on realistic concerns, whereas anxiety is often based on nothing at all or mentally fabricated concerns.

- Worry can often be controlled and managed, but anxiety is harder to get rid of.

- Worry does not prevent us from living our life; anxiety will interfere personally and professionally.

- Worry is based on a very specific concern, whereas anxiety is more general.

- Worry is often something we think about mentally, whereas anxiety is felt mentally and physically.

Once you can identify if what you are feeling is worry or anxiety, you will be better equipped to handle it since each is treated differently. When you are worried about something, that is okay, and you will be able to handle it on your own and at the moment. Anxiety, on the other hand, is less easy to deal with and can oftentimes require professional help or even medication (which we will get into later on in this book).

What Does Anxiety Look Like?

Anxiety can be broken down into three main components: thoughts, sensations, and actions. These three components are experienced by those who are having healthy anxiety, but it is also experienced by those who are having unhealthy anxiety. The difference between the two comes down to this:

- Unhealthy anxiety happens and you do not know why.
- It is not a situation where most people would feel anxious.
- The anxiety lingers even after the situation has passed.
- You change the way you behave because of the anxiety.

If you can identify one or more of these during an anxiety attack, then you can know that you are experiencing unhealthy anxiety. So, what will that feel like to you?

Unhealthy Anxious Thoughts

The first component you will experience is the thoughts that plague your mind. These are thoughts that are unwanted and yet refuse to go away. You may be anxious that:

- Something you said or could say has upset someone.
- You do not have control over your environment or surroundings.
- That you are going to be late, or early, to a meeting.
- That something is about to go wrong.
- You have forgotten something important.
- The future may always be on your mind.
- You may feel like everyone is mad at you.
- Fear of embarrassment in public.
- Anxiety about making a mistake and being judged.
- You may feel anxious about feeling anxious.

These are all thoughts that something bad is going to happen, is happening, or has happened, and you cannot stop thinking about it. Whether or not there is any truth to the situation is irrelevant because, in your mind, it is very much real.

Unhealthy Anxiety Sensations

Anxiety has a physical component to it, as it is not just mental but can also create various physical sensations that are unpleasant and overwhelming. Some of the sensations that are associated with unhealthy anxiety include:

- Feeling like your heart is racing
- Heavy and quick breathing
- Sweaty palms
- Dizziness or lightheadedness
- Nausea or stomach pain
- Headaches and neck tension
- Shaking and shivering
- Difficulty falling asleep or staying asleep

The physical sensations are a big component because it makes it feel that much more real. When our bodies react in such a way, it tells us that what we are thinking is justified and it reaffirms that we need to be on alert and ready. These symptoms can also make us significantly more anxious because they are a signal to others that something is wrong with us. When it is just mental symptoms, we can hide those more easily, but if we are shaking and sweating, then someone may ask us what is wrong. This is why people with anxiety avoid being around others as it can make the cycle worse.

Unhealthy Anxiety Actions

When our mind and body tell us something is very wrong or something bad is about to happen, we will then respond by taking action to protect ourselves.

Many of us have heard the term "fight-or-flight" before, and that is typically what occurs during an anxiety attack. Even if it isn't real, we now perceive a situation as being an attack on us, so we respond accordingly to escape danger. Some common unhealthy anxiety actions include:

- We may act out and snap at those around us.

- We may avoid certain situations.

- We may freeze up and be unable to function.

- We may hideaway in our homes and not go outside.

- We may cut off contact with loved ones.

- We may engage in unhealthy self-medicating behaviors such as consuming alcohol or drugs.

- We may become overly dependent on a spouse or loved one.

- We may avoid places that we think will trigger us such as public transportation, school, or even work.

This is the aspect of anxiety that interferes with our day-to-day life because we can no longer function normally. Instead of getting up each day and going to work, we become anxious to the point where basic tasks suddenly seem overwhelming. When anxiety gets to this point, that is when most of us start to realize that it is a serious problem that requires help.

Causes of Fears, Anxiety and Panic Attacks

Anxiety

The time and how intense the feeling of anxiety is can sometimes be extensive as compared to the trigger. When the anxiety feeling exceeds, a person may experience increased blood pressure, and feelings of nausea may develop. When the feelings are this intense, they move from being normal anxiety to being an anxiety disorder.

A person that has an anxiety disorder is described as one with persistent concerns or thoughts that are intrusive. When a person cannot function normally due to anxious feelings, the person is considered to be suffering from an anxiety disorder.

Symptoms that an individual is suffering from an anxiety disorder

Various symptoms constitute to a person having an anxiety disorder. Some of these symptoms of the generalized disorder will include:

- An individual feeling restless and on edge
- When a person has feelings of worry that are uncontrollable
- When a person becomes increasingly irritable
- When a person experiences difficulties in concentration
- When a person starts experiencing difficulties falling asleep or sleeping in general

Although these may seem like normal symptoms that are common, individuals with a generalized anxiety disorder (GAD) experience them at extreme levels.

With GAD, a person has vague, unsettling concerns and in some cases, severe anxiety that disrupts the daily functioning of the individual.

Common Causes of Anxiety Attacks

Causes of anxiety disorders are varied and complicated. Some causes may happen at the same time; others may lead to others, while others may not result in anxiety disorder unless another cause is present.

Some possible causes are:

- Environmental triggers such as challenges at work, family issues or relationship issues
- Genetics. Individuals that have family members that suffer from anxiety disorders could also experience them too.
- Medical triggers like symptoms of other diseases, the side effect of medication, the stress of an impending surgery, or recovery that has been prolonged.
- Brain chemistry meaning there is a misalignment of hormones and signals to the brain
- Withdrawing from taking an illicit substance may cause an intense impact on other triggers.

Physical and mental Clutter as a cause of Anxiety

Many people have accumulated many things in their lives that have caused clutter both in their physical environment and their minds. Clutter is a major cause of anxiety. A person bombards themselves with more material things than is necessary as well as having clutter in the mind. Living a simple life is a great way to avoid clutter, both mentally and physically, that would otherwise overwhelm you and cause you anxiety.

Many people want to please others, and they end up promising more than they can deliver. This will definitely cause you mental stress that makes you have anxious feelings. To prevent or avoid and even treat anxiety symptoms, people need to evaluate themselves and understand the clutter they are carrying and how to avoid it.

Fear

At the root of all mental disorders is one critical element known as fear. When it seizes your mind and body, you can only take one direction: down.

Fear is what will cause you to be scared of talking in front of an audience, what will hold you back from asking a member of the opposite sex out on a date, and what will make you shocked when you take an exam. But let's be clear. Fear is not wholly bad. Actually, it's a survival weapon that conditions us to perceive threats within our vicinity and react by either fighting back or escaping.

Anxiety is a type of fear that is tied to the thought of a threat or something terrible happening in the future as opposed to now. A person with an anxiety disorder battles intrusive and obsessive thoughts, as they try to make sense of both their emotions and thoughts.

What Makes You Afraid?

There are very many things that drive us into fear. The origins of our fear are, for the most part, rooted in our childhood experiences. If our guardians instill a fear of darkness in our childhood, we will grow into adults who still fear darkness until the moment we challenge that irrational fear. The first step toward overcoming fear is becoming aware of what you're afraid of and why.

What Makes You Anxious?

Anxiety is merely persistent fear, and it extends to your future. Having an anxiety disorder will surely harm your quality of life. You get into the mindset of seeing problems where there are none. Anxiety puts a quality of extremity to your life so that you're either withdrawn and isolated, or aggressive. Both extremes tend to stifle social cohesion.

How Does Fear Manifest?

When you are frightened or anxious, both your body and mind operate too quick. The following are some of the things that may happen thanks to fear and anxiety:

- Increased heartbeat
- Increased rate of breathing
- Weak muscles
- Profuse sweating
- Stomach pains
- Lack of concentration
- Lightheadedness
- A feeling of getting frozen

- Loss of appetite
- Hot and cold sweats
- Tense muscles
- Dry mouth

The physical symptoms of fear can be very frustrating, especially if you have no idea about the cause of your fear or anxiety. There are various triggers for fear and, sometimes, the brain keeps sending these messages even unnecessarily. You can only improve your capacity to understand your relationship with fear by raising your self-awareness.

Panic Attacks

Panic attack can be described as a sudden onset of extreme fear that continually increases for a couple of minutes. When you have a panic attack, you just experience overwhelming fear and anxiety coming over you, but you may not really understand what is happening.

You feel as if you are about to die from a heart attack due to the accelerated heart rate and other intense symptoms. However, you are experiencing the attack because of some psychological factors. A panic attack usually lasts for about 15 to 20 minutes, so the most important thing to do is to ride it out and wait for your body to go back to normal.

You may think that panic attacks are rare, but the truth is that they are quite common, with women being more susceptible than men. Though it is possible to experience a panic attack at any age, the majority of people tend to start feeling the effects between the ages of 25 and 30.

Symptoms

For you to be considered to be suffering from a panic attack, you must experience four or more of the following symptoms:

- Sweating
- Heart palpitations (increased heart rate)
- Trembling
- Shortness of breath
- Choking sensations
- Chest pain
- Feeling chilly or hot
- Light-headedness
- Abdominal discomfort
- Feeling like you are losing control
- Fear of dying
- Tingling or numb sensations

Causes

A panic attack is primarily the result of the adrenaline hormone flooding the body due to perceived danger. Notice that the key word here is perceived, which means that the problem is psychological in nature. As your adrenaline levels increase, you experience the above symptoms, but the hormone cannot stay at that high level for long, and soon drops down to normal.

Other factors that may contribute to your panic attacks include drinking too much coffee, stress, or failure to get adequate sleep. Maybe it was an impending exam or bad news about a loved one's health. Knowledge the cause will help you know what factors to avoid and reduce your anxiety about experiencing an attack when you least expect it.

Identifying Obstacles Works with Thoughts, Worry, Fears and Anxiety

One of the greatest joys of my life is being able to help people overcome their anxiety and depression naturally. I'm sharing this knowledge with you today because I'd love to see you transform your life more easily than I did. I know you're going to love experiencing emotional health and happiness!

Yet, with anything that is precious and valuable in life, there are challenges and roadblocks to overcome along the way. So, of course there are also some problems and challenges with overcoming anxiety and depression naturally.

Let's discuss some of these challenges and roadblocks, so that you have a better understanding of the healing process.

Roadblock #1: Giving in to the conventional belief system

When we are feeling lost, scared and alone, it's very easy for us to believe the current conventional beliefs that say we are permanently damaged and we need medication to function normally.

Remember that we are programmed to believe those things by the multi-billion dollar corporations who are primarily concerned with marketing their medications. The well-being of consumers appears to be secondary to them.

Roadblock #2: Not having a mentor or guide

Since most of us were not taught how to resolve our feelings, it can often be a challenge to find our way through the muddle of our unresolved emotional issues on our own. Even if our intentions are good, we may feel lost and confused while trying to sort out complex issues by ourselves.

Fortunately, the truth about our life is actually simple. When we are guided appropriately, we can learn simple methods to find our way through the quagmire of unresolved issues and into the light of inner peace and happiness!

Roadblock #3: No support system for emotional health

Most of us didn't have healthy role models for emotional health as children. As a result, we generally copied the unhealthy family patterns we grew up with. When we don't have adequate support for getting out of our unhealthy family system, we can easily get distracted and lose track of our goals.

Learning how to find support for our personal growth can make all the difference in achieving health and happiness. By developing a healthy support system, we can always have someone to talk to on the days that we really need support for our healing journey.

Roadblock #4: Having a lack of patience, commitment and persistence

Facing the truth about your life does have its challenges. Without these important qualities, it's easy to get derailed by the twists and turns that come on our journey to emotional health.

When we are working through difficult life issues, we'll probably have days where our emotions feel overwhelming. But when we practice our patience, commitment and persistence, often those challenging days mark the beginning of an amazing breakthrough in our lives.

Roadblock #5: Giving up before you complete the journey

Some people start the process and then decide it's too hard or it takes too long, so they go back to their old behaviors and wonder why their life isn't working.

If we give up before we get to emotional health and happiness, we miss out on experiencing the amazing happiness and inner peace that are possible.

Triumph Over Anger and Depression

Anger usually occurs as a natural response to feeling attacked, frustrated, or even being humiliated. It is human nature to get angry. The fury, therefore, is not a bad feeling per se, because, at times, it can prove to be very useful. How is this even possible? Anger can open one's mind and help them identify their problems, which could drive one to get motivated to make a change, which could help in molding their lives.

When is Anger a Problem?

Anger, as we have just seen, is normal in life. The problem only comes in when one cannot manage their anger, and it causes harm to people around them or even themselves.

How does one notice when their anger is becoming harmful? When one starts expressing anger through unhelpful or destructive behavior, or even when one's mental and physical health starts deteriorating. That's when one knows that the situation is getting out of hand.

It is the way a person behaves that determines whether or not they have problems with their anger. If the way they act affects their life or relationships, then there is a problem, and they should think about getting some support or treatment.

What is Unhelpful Angry Behavior?

Anger may be familiar to everyone, but people usually express their rage in entirely different ways. How one behaves when they are angry depends on how much control they have over their feelings. People who have less control over their emotions tend to have some unhelpful angry behaviors. These are behaviors that cause damage to themselves or even damage to people or things around them. They include:

Inward Aggression

This is where one directs their anger towards themselves. Some of the behaviors here may include telling oneself that they hate themselves, denying themselves, or even cutting themselves off the world.

Non-Violent or Passive Aggression

In this case, one does not direct their anger anywhere; rather, they stick with the feeling in them. Some of the behaviors here may include ignoring people, refusing to speak to people, refusing to do tasks, or even deliberately doing chores poorly or late. These types of behaviors are usually the worst ways to approach such situations. They may seem less destructive and harmful, but they do not relieve one of the heavy burdens that are causing them to be angry.

Preparation

Weigh Your Options

In life, many things may be out of one's control. These things vary from the weather, the past, other people, intrusive thoughts, physical sensations, and one's own emotions. Despite all these, the power to choose is always disposable to any human. Even though one might not be able to control the weather, one can decide whether or not to wear heavy clothing. One can also choose how to respond to other people.

The first step, therefore, in dealing with anger is to recognize a choice.

Steps to Take in Managing Anger

1. A "Should" Rule is Broken

Everybody has some rules and expectations for one's behavior, and also for other people's behavior. Some of these rules include, "I should be able to do this," "She should not treat me like this," and, "They should stay out of my way." Unfortunately, no one has control over someone else's actions. Therefore, these rules are always bound to be broken, and people may get in one's way. This can result in anger, guilt, and pressure.

It is, therefore, essential to the first break these "should" rules to fight this anger. The first step to make in breaking these rules is to accept the reality of life that someone usually has very little control over other people's lives. The next step is for one to choose a direction based on one's values. How does one know their values? One can identify their values by what angers them, frustrates them, or even enrages them. For example, let's take the rule of "They should stay out of my way." This rule may mean the values of communication, progress, or even cooperation. What do these values mean to someone? Does one have control over them?

Finally, one can act by their values. To help with this, here are two questions one should ask themselves:

- What does one want in the long run?
- What constructive steps can one take in that direction?

2. What Hurts?

The second step is to find the real cause of pain or fear after breaking the rules. These rules usually do not mean the same as one's body. This is because some states of being can hurt one's self-esteem more than others.

To understand this better, let's take the example of Susan, who expects that no one should talk ill of her. Then suddenly John comes up to her and says all manner of things to her. This, therefore, makes Susan enraged. In such a scenario, Susan should ask herself what hurts her. The answer to this question will bring out a general belief about John and herself. She will think that "John is rude," "She is powerless," or even that "She is being made the victim." All these thoughts may hurt her. What may even hurt her most is that she has no control over John's behavior.

Once she has noted that she has no control, she may now consider seeing John's words as a mere opinion rather than an insult. This will make her not see herself as a victim, but as a person just receiving a piece of someone else's mind about herself.

3. Hot Thoughts.

After one has identified what really hurts them, it is now time to identify and, most importantly, replace the hot, anger-driven, and reactive thoughts with more level-headed, more relaxed, and reflective thoughts. Here are some fresh ideas that may be of importance to someone:

Hot thought: "How mean can he be!"

A cool thought: "He thinks he is so caring."

Hot thought: "They are stupid!"

A cool thought: "They are just human."

4. Anger

All the above steps, as one may have noticed, relate to the thoughts. This is because one has first to tackle the ideas before now getting to the emotion. In this step, therefore, one is going to respond to the anger arousal itself. There are three ways that one can follow to respond to this emotion:

- One may indulge in relaxation. This relaxation can come in many forms, like enjoying some music, practicing some progressive muscle relaxation like yoga, and also visualization.

- One may also use that feeling to do some constructive work. When one is angry, there is usually a large amount of energy that one uses at that time. This is the reason that when angry, one can break down things that they would never break when calm. Imagine, therefore, how much that energy would do for someone if just directed to some constructive work.

- One may also try to redefine anger when one gets angry. What does this mean? Once a person is angry, one can try to remind themselves of how anger is a problem that fuels aggression and can cause harm to loved ones and even oneself.

5. Moral Disengagement

In simple words, this step will help one examine the beliefs that turn anger into aggression. These beliefs usually act as mere excuses or justification for destructive acts. Some of these beliefs include "I don't care," "This is the only way I can get my point across," or even "It is high time they recognize me." These beliefs need to be identified early enough and gotten rid of before they can con one into throwing one's morals aside. One sure way of getting rid of them is by reminding oneself of the cost of such beliefs and the advantages of striving for understanding.

6. Aggression

In this step, one now needs to examine the behaviors that arise from aggression and try to fight them. Fighting these behaviors can be achieved if one calms down and puts themselves in the other person's shoes. This will help one understand why the other person is acting in such a manner, what they may be feeling, or even what they may be thinking. This approach will help to:

- Decrease the anger for all parties involved.
- Increase the chance of having a reasonable conversation with the parties involved, and thus everybody is heard.

7. Outcome

The final step of this procedure is to reduce resentment towards others, and also guilt towards oneself.

Treating depression with cognitive behavioral therapy.

What is depression?

Depression is a feeling of severe despondency and dejection. In life, it is only natural for one to feel less than a hundred percent at times. This is like when one is battling with drug addiction or has relationship problems. However, this low feeling sometimes gets a hold of one's life and won't go. This is what we call depression. Depression can make one feel lonely and hopeless.

If one has such feelings, there is light at the end of the tunnel. Cognitive Behavioral Therapy is here to restore one's hope in life. This is because it can help one think more healthily, and also help in overcoming a particular addiction.

Before getting more in-depth with the advantages of CBT on a depressed person, let's first look at the different types of depression.

Types of Depression

Depressions are of various kinds. They can either occur alone or concurrently with an addiction. The best thing, however, is that the following categories are treatable through using CBT.

Major Depression

This disorder occurs when one feels depressed most of the time for most days of the week. Some of the symptoms associated with this disorder are:

- Weight loss or weight gain
- Being tired often
- Trouble getting sleep
- Thoughts of suicide
- Concentration problems
- Feeling restless or agitated

If you experience five or more of the above signs on most days for two weeks or longer, then they have this disorder.

Persistent Depressive Disorder (PDD)

This type of depression usually lasts for two years or even longer. The symptoms associated with the disorder include:

- Sleeping too much or too little
- Fatigue
- Low self-esteem

Bipolar Disorder

A person with such a disorder usually experiences mood episodes that range from extremes of high energy with an "up" mood to low periods.

How CBT Helps with Negative Thoughts of Depression

The cognitive-behavioral therapy understands that when one has low moods, they tend to have negative thinking. This negative thinking usually brings cases of hopelessness, depression, and can also lead to a change in behavior.

CBT, therefore, works to help with the patterns of behavior that need to be changed. In short, it works to recalibrate the part of the brain that keeps a tight hold on happy thoughts.

Five CBT Techniques to Counteract the Negative Thinking of Depression

There are several techniques that one can follow to help with fighting off negative thoughts. Before starting these steps, one should make sure that they are ready to undertake them and should keep track of themselves. Here are some of the steps:

Locate the Problem and Brainstorm for Solutions

The first step is to discover the cause of the problem. This step requires one to talk with one's inner self. Once the idea of what the problem might be dawning on you, write it down in simple words. Then write down a list of things that one can do to improve the problem.

Write Self-Statements to Counteract Negative Thoughts

Once the cause of the problem has been discovered, it is now time to identify the negative thoughts that seem to pop up in one's brain every time. Write self-statements to counteract each foul view. These self-statements are statements that are going to stuff up the negative thoughts. One should always recall all their self-statements and repeat them back to themselves every time a negative thought pops up. However, these self-statements should continually be refreshed because they can, at times, be too routine.

Find New Opportunities to Think Positive Thoughts

Michael is a person who always sees the negative part of people before noticing their bright side. These people, more often than not, usually get depressed quickly. To remedy this, they should always change their thinking and think positively. This, for example, in the case of Michael, can be like first noticing and appreciating how neat people are. This type of thinking can be tough to change. Here are some of the recommended ways that one can adjust to such thinking;

- Set one's phone to remind them to reframe their minds to something positive.

- Pairing up with someone who is working on this same technique. This will make one have positive thoughts, and also get to enjoy them with someone else.

Finish Each Day by Visualizing Its Best Parts

After each day, one can write down the most exciting events of the day and try to remember them. Sharing such moments online can even help one form new associations, and also thinking ways that can prove to be very helpful.

Learn to Accept Disappointment as a Normal Part of Life

In life, disappointment is bound to come one's way. How one deals or behaves after a disappointing event determines how fast one is going to move forward. Take, for example, John, who just lost a job interview. This is a thing that can happen to anyone. The way he responds to this situation will determine how fast he is going to move forward. If he starts getting the thoughts of "I am a failure," "The world is so unfair to me," or even "I will never succeed in life," then he is moving in the wrong direction. Later, he can write some things he has learned from the experience and things he can do to remedy it next time.

Challenging Automatic and Intrusive Thoughts

Cognitive reconstruction in CBT for anxiety

Cognitive reconstruction also referred to as thought challenging involves a process whereby we simply challenge the patterns yielding to negative thoughts.

The goal of doing this is to make you anxious and then replacing these patterns with realistic and positive thinking. Here are the steps involved in doing this are;

Identification of the negative thoughts

People suffering from anxiety disorders perceive situations that we see to be normal as very dangerous. For example, germ phobia can make someone to really find it life-threatening when shaking another person's hands. In as much as it may appear easy to see the irrational fears, it can, however, be difficult to identify your own irrational and scary thoughts. Therefore, the most preferred strategy is by asking yourself to roll back to determine your thoughts at the moment the anxiety feeling started. You should be guided on how to do this step by step by your therapist.

Challenging the negative thoughts in you

You have already identified the thoughts that make you anxious. Therefore, your therapist will provide you with a guide on how you can evaluate the thoughts that provoke your anxiety. This will basically involve trying to question the evidence of thoughts that frighten you, analyzing of beliefs you feel are unhelpful and then trying to test the reality of negative predictions. In order to effectively challenge your negative thoughts, you can conduct experiments, weigh the advantages and disadvantages of worrying and then try to determine the realistic chances of the possibilities of what you are worrying or anxious about.

Negative thinking is something that everyone does from time to time, however, those suffering from depression are at risk for being controlled by it. It influences your decisions and has a major impact on your mood. When you fall into negative thinking, it also makes it a lot harder to fight your depression, so it is important to get this type of thinking under control.

The first step is identifying your negative thoughts so that you can work to counter them and turn them into something positive. When you start to feel emotions like anger, frustration, irritability, depressed mood or anxiousness, take a minute to think about why you feel this way. This gives you a minute to reflect on what is happening and what is causing these emotions. You want to do four things what you are experiencing negative emotions to identify your negative thoughts and overcome them:

Test Reality

Test the reality of your negative thoughts by asking yourself the following:

• What evidence supports my current thinking?

• Am I jumping to a negative conclusion?

• Are my thoughts interpretations or are they factual?

• How can I determine if these thoughts are true?

Seek Alternative Explanations

Ask yourself these questions to see if there are alternative explanations:

• What could this mean?

• What other ways can I explore this situation?

• How would I see this situation if I were being positive?

Put it in Perspective

Put your thinking and feelings in perspective by asking yourself these questions:

• Is this situation really as bad as I see it?

• What great things can happen in this situation?

• What is good about this situation?

• Will this situation even matter in five years?

• How likely is something bad to happen and what is the worst that can happen?

• What is likely to happen?

Utilize Goal-Directed Thinking

Ask yourself the following questions to take advantage of goal-directed thinking:

• Are my thoughts helping me to reach my goals?

• Can I learn something from this situation?

• What can I do to solve the problem?

These four steps allow you to work through your negative thoughts so that you can explore their origin so that you can prevent them in the future. When you recognize negative thoughts and take the time to address them, you are working toward thinking more positively naturally. This means that you will be less likely to experience negative thoughts in the future. You will gain a new perspective and be able to use it effectively to transform your thoughts into something that helps you to move forward.

There are four other things that you can do to work toward challenging your negative thoughts and feelings. Consider the following methods for helping you to think more positively:

• Talk it out: Find someone who you trust who knows you well and talk about your negative thoughts and feelings. The key to talking about it with someone else is to get a fresh perspective to help you understand, recognize and undo your negative thinking.

• Get relaxed: Take a few minutes each day and do something relaxing that allows you to get inside your own head and consider your thoughts. Things like meditation and yoga are popular options because they help you to open your mind so that you can focus on the thoughts that you are having.

• Improve your physical health: When you are working on your physical health, this often boosts your confidence. Those with more confidence tend to naturally think more positively. This also gives you positive things in your life to focus on.

• Write it down: When you are having negative thoughts, take a minute to write them down. You can look at them later in the day to determine where your negative thoughts were coming from. This will allow you to make the changes necessary to become a more positive person. It also helps you to identify that factors that cause you to have negative thoughts.

Replacing the negative thoughts

Now that the negative distortions and irrational predictions have been identified, it is time now you replace such thoughts with more positive and accurate thoughts. In such situations, you can let your therapist assist you in developing for you new realistic thoughts or motivating statements that you can always refer to when faced with a tough situation that normally makes you anxious.

Let's consider the following examples: Bill is afraid of taking a subway because he feels that he will pass out, and everybody in the sub will think that he is crazy. He decides to go for therapy. The therapist, in turn, asked him to think and write down his negative thoughts and then try to identify the cognitive distortions or the errors that he feels are in his thinking. After doing this, the therapist told him to develop a rational interpretation of his thoughts.

Challenging the Negative Thoughts in You

The first thought (negative): I will faint while on the subway. What will happen if that happens?

Cognitive distortion: Prediction of the worst

Realistic thinking: This has never happened to me. This will not happen.

ii. The second negative thought: It will really be terrible if I pass out

Cognitive distortion: Things are already blowing out of control

Realistic thinking: The subway has its own medics and therefore if I faint, that will not be terrible

iii. The third negative thought: Other people will definitely think of me as crazy

Cognitive distortion: You are already jumping into conclusions

Realistic thinking: People will be concerned to see that I get okay

Replacing the negative thoughts, however, is not easy. This is because negative thinking forms part and parcel of a prolonged thinking pattern and will require time and practice to break this bad habit. For this reason, cognitive behavioral therapy also includes practicing where you are required to as well as practice while at home.

Taking Action Against Anxiety

When you are stuck in depression, you may feel like you cannot progress.

What are Action Plans?

Action plans are another way to engage in problem-solving. These involve six specific questions that you must consider in regards to whatever it is that you are trying to get, and if you can answer them, you have a pretty good plan to get what you need.

These action plans can help you understand what comes next when you are trying to get what you want. By breaking down your goal into manageable steps, you will understand how to get there without getting overwhelmed.

The whole purpose of action plans, beyond just creating steps, is to push you from someone who has things that happen to you into a doer. You are no longer going to be a passive part of your life—instead, you are learning how to take action and do something.

How do Action Plans Help Depression?

When you suffer from depression, you likely feel like you are all caught up in the world around you, feeling like there is little to no point in moving on. You do not see the point in changing your own behaviors because you feel like it will not matter anyway.

You may even be too overwhelmed to actually tackle your problem in the first place. This can be problematic for you if stress is one of your biggest depression triggers. However, you do not have to be overwhelmed any longer. As you come up with an action plan, you create manageable steps to achieving what you want. Because the steps will be smaller and more manageable than the entire goal as a whole, you will not feel nearly as intimidated by it. This means that you will have more luck actually engaging with your action plan and getting what you want.

Steps to Creating Action Plans

When it comes time to create an action plan, you must first start off with a problem. After all, your action plan would not be complete without a problem that it seeks to solve, or a goal that you wish to achieve. Perhaps you are stressed about school and wish to alleviate that stress. Maybe you stress because you have a tendency to snap at your children, and the fact that you do snap at them just makes your stress level worsen. Those are both emotional issues, which action plans can help you with. You can develop strategies to lessen the stress. However, you can also create action plans in other contexts as well.

Perhaps you want to lose some weight or develop a new skill. Your action plan can help you with that. You might want to learn how to be more social, which can also be done through action planning. You may even need to find a new job or wish to get into a relationship with someone else. That is also entirely possible for you to achieve with action plans.

Ultimately, your action plan is going to help you achieve whatever it is you desire. Your action plan is going to ask you six specific questions that can help you really flesh out what it is you want. As you go through these six questions, you will get a better understanding of everything that your action goal entails.

First, identify what you want and write it down. This is anything you want. In this case, let's use the example of wanting to get a new job. That is something that is nice and concrete, making it easy to understand.

Next, you are going to ask yourself why it is important. In this case, you need a new job. This is relatively simple to understand why you would need one—everyone needs money. You may need the pay raise that would come with a new job, or perhaps you are miserable at your current job and need out for your own sanity. Maybe your job is something boring to you, and you want to pursue a field that will make you happier. You may even want to relocate but relocating requires you to first land a job wherever you would like to move.

Now, ask yourself when you want this to happen. This is creating a timeline for your action. This is important because if you never have a timeline for it, you are not going to feel particularly pressured to attempt to get your desired result. When you do have a timeline, however, you are able to keep yourself accountable. This accountability can be the difference between failing or succeeding.

Third, ask what you need in order to achieve your goal. Do you need any new skills to get that new job you want? Is going back to college or getting a new certification necessary? Do you need a car that will enable you to get to and from your dream job? Do you need to relocate? Will you need a change in the wardrobe to match the new job's company culture?

Fourth, identify if you need any intervention from other people, or if you could benefit from asking someone else to help. Do you have any references for that job you want? Is there anyone you can talk to that already works for the company that you want to work for that can give you an idea of what to expect? Do you need a babysitter for kids while you interview or start at your new job?

Fifth, you need to ask yourself how you will know that you have actually achieved the goal. In this case, that is quite simple: You will have a new job. Sometimes, however, things are not as clear. You may want to reduce your depression's effect on you, and that is something that can be difficult to really measure. However, you can say that you know you have achieved that goal when you are able to face your daily responsibilities most of the time.

Lastly, you now start planning out the steps. What are the steps you will need to reach your goal? With applying for a job, it is relatively simple; once more— you will need to locate jobs that are hiring at that moment, create a resume and cover letter, ensure you have references, apply, interview, and accept a job offer. When you want to alleviate some of your depressive symptoms, you may say that you will engage in therapy, increase your healthy behaviors, take antidepressants, and find any other ways that you could help alleviate those depressive symptoms.

With all of your actions lined up for you to consider, you are able to see exactly what your goal is going to require. When you are suffering from depression, you want your goals to be as clear-cut as possible, allowing you to take action in a way that does not seem intimidating to you. After all, if you feel like the process is insurmountable or like you cannot succeed because you do not know where to start, you are not likely to get very far.

To help you with your action planning, it can help to create a list or a graphic that makes everything visible for you as you go through the planning period. As you finish the action plan graphic, you will be able to see everything in front of you as you organize it, which ensures that you do not forget parts along the way. You will have all of your brainstorming right in front of you so you can get it right the first time.

When you create a web-like the above one, you are actively putting in the effort necessary to plan. Sometimes, that planning can be enough to spur you into action, as you feel like going through the effort and writing it down commits you to finish. After all, why would you have gone through that effort if you were not going to use it? If you do not want to waste time, you will be committed to acting. This is frequently known as the sunk-cost fallacy, where you feel like the resources you have invested justify following the process through to the end. Usually, this is something that can be detrimental to you, particularly if you have put in money to a business and are now at risk of losing it if you continue to invest and having your credit ruined, or if you stick out a relationship in which you are miserable because you have been together for too long to not try. However, when you use an action plan to trigger that, you can use what is usually a negative as a positive instead, taking advantage of the way that minds tend to function and using it to your benefit.

Releasing Control

One of the biggest benefits behind managing anxiety with CBT is that you are managing your anxiety in a natural way. While some forms of anxiety will require medication, some people find that creating a natural management plan is much easier and feels more aligned with them and their needs. With that being said, CBT is not the only way that you can manage your anxiety in a natural manner that will help improve your symptoms and support you with feeling your best. If you want to really approach your anxiety with a full system for helping you not only manage but also heal and cure your anxiety, incorporating some alternative natural approaches can be helpful, too.

When it comes to anxiety, specifically, there are several things you can do to help you begin to manage your anxiety more effectively. Most of these methods are lifestyle methods, although some of them can be targeted toward anxiety itself, too. The eight things that you can do that will really help you navigate your anxiety more effectively and naturally heal yourself include: exercise, avoiding anxiety-inducing substances, resting, meditating, improving your diet, teas, and herbs, aromatherapy, and taking the pressure off of yourself.

Maintain Regular Exercise

Exercise is necessary for your general wellbeing, yet many people fail to incorporate enough exercise into their everyday routine. Ideally, you should be engaging in at least 30 minutes of moderate exercise every single day, as well as moving your body around at least once per hour. Ensuring that you engage in enough movement and exercise will help you use up any adrenaline and cortisol that your body may produce as a byproduct of your anxiety. As well, it will help naturally regulate your hormones and chemicals to ensure that your hormonal system is functioning more effectively. For some people, this can translate to experiencing less anxiety overall because their system functions more effectively as a result of their exercise.

In addition to helping you regulate your hormones and chemicals within your body, exercise can also release endorphins into your system that actually support you in staying more relaxed and navigating anxiety, as well as other emotions more effectively. These endorphins can be found in your body for up to several hours after working out, meaning that one single workout session can help regulate your hormones, chemicals, and emotions for several hours. If you continue working out on a consistent basis, this can translate to ongoing, long-term relief from your anxiety symptoms.

Avoid Alcohol, Cigarettes, and Caffeine

Alcohol is known for being a natural sedative, which means that it can support you with relaxing yourself from anxiety. One single glass of wine or a shot of whiskey can calm your nerves and support you with navigating your anxiety more effectively – at first. However, as soon as the buzz from that small portion of alcohol wears off, your anxiety can come back far stronger and more intense than ever. Attempting to treat your anxiety with alcohol can lead to alcoholism while also exacerbating the symptoms of your anxiety and making you feel even worse in the long run.

Cigarettes are also known for exacerbating your anxiety by worsening your risk of anxiety over time. Although smoking a cigarette when you are actively feeling stressed might seem to calm you down, the reality is that research has shown that long-term cigarette usage actually massively increases your risk for problematic anxiety symptoms. As well, nicotine itself is said to increase your anxiety symptoms, which means that you may actually find yourself feeling even worse after a cigarette.

Lastly, caffeine is known as a stimulant and can massively aggravate your anxiety. If you are drinking caffeine on a regular basis, and you find yourself dealing with problematic anxiety, you need to start cutting back on caffeine or eliminating it entirely. Releasing caffeine from your daily drinking ritual will massively support you with avoiding unwanted anxiety and allowing yourself to experience more calmness in your life.

Create A Stronger Rest Routine

People who experience chronic or problematic anxiety often report that they tend to experience a strange or inconsistent sleep schedule. For some people, the strange or inconsistent sleep schedule might be the result of their anxiety itself, whereas others might find that the schedule is more closely linked to their lifestyle and leads to the experience of anxiety. If you are trying to overcome anxiety in your life, learning how to navigate a healthier rest cycle will be important to your wellbeing. The more you can support yourself in navigating a healthier rest cycle, the more you will find yourself experiencing freedom from your anxiety.

Ideally, you should have a strong bedtime routine as well as plenty of sleep throughout each night to support you with experiencing healthier rest cycles and more support from your sleep. With both in place, you will likely find yourself experiencing significant relief from your anxiety.

For your bedtime routine, try avoiding using your phone, tablet, or any other device with a screen for at least 30-45 minutes before bed. As well, do not read or watch television in bed or otherwise engage in active activities in your bed as this can lead to you associating your bed with a space to be active and awake. You should also try incorporating some relaxing pre-bedtime routines, like drinking a relaxing tea, journaling, taking a warm bath, or doing a gentle yoga practice. These types of calming experiences will help you release your stress, calm your mind, and prepare yourself for a good night's sleep.

You should also make sure that you are going to bed at a reasonable hour and waking up 7-9 hours later, which is the recommended amount of sleep for the average adult. Getting a proper amount of sleep and waking up on time will ensure that you are well-rested when you wake up and that you have not overslept, too.

Practice Meditating

Meditation is one of the most powerful things you can do to help you naturally relieve anxiety, and it can also support you with active anxiety attacks or bouts of anxiety if you find yourself struggling. Having a regular meditation practice will support you with relaxing yourself in between anxiety, and with managing your anxiety more effectively and completely when it spikes. Your main goal with meditation is to relax your mind and let yourself experience peace, so naturally, this can have a positive and healthy impact on your mind, especially when you are navigating anxiety. In fact, some studies have shown that those who meditate on a consistent basis experience massive relief from things such as anxiety, stress, worry, and even depression and other emotional or mental disorders.

If you are new to meditation, getting into the practice of meditating for just 10-15 minutes per day can have a huge impact on helping you relieve yourself from anxiety. However, you should be focused on working your way up to meditating for about 30 minutes a day, as this is what John Hopkins medical research center recommends as being the best length of time for relief from anxiety, as well as depression. You should practice meditating whether you feel anxious or not, as keeping a healthy and ongoing meditation practice will support you in fully overcoming anxiety in the long run. Think of this as being similar to practicing CBT techniques outside of anxiety before bringing them into your anxiety cycle: the more you practice, the better you get, and the more effective it will be at helping you in your times of need.

If you struggle to meditate, following a guided meditation on YouTube can be helpful in allowing you to meditate more effectively. You may also want to turn meditation into more of a ritual where you involve gentle music, a comfortable pillow and blanket, and some soothing aromatherapy or candles to help set the tone. The more you can relax and let your mind experience relief, the more peace you will experience in your life.

Improve Your Diet

Much like alcohol, cigarettes, and caffeine can impact your anxiety, and your diet can actually impact your anxiety, too. Your diet can increase symptoms of anxiety in many ways. If you are not eating enough or you are not eating well enough, your body can become stressed from your unhealthy dietary styles and can actually increase your levels of cortisol in your body, which can lead to symptoms of anxiety. As well, some foods are naturally energizing and can lead to you having anxiety as a result of these boosted energies. Learning to avoid any form of natural stimulants can be helpful in supporting you with navigating your anxiety more effectively.

The foods you need to avoid include any that have been processed or that are laced in chemicals such as artificial flavors, colors, or preservatives. You also need to avoid letting your blood sugars drop too low or letting yourself get dehydrated, as these can both lead to the increase of anxiety within your body. In addition to that, avoid high sugar diets and stimulating foods and herbs like ginseng, chocolate (which can contain caffeine), and any other number of herbs or supplements that may be stimulating in nature.

Eating a diet that is healthy and rich in complex carbohydrates, vegetables, fruits, and lean proteins can help you support yourself with overcoming anxiety more effectively. You can also focus on eating foods that are known for supporting your brain health, such as those that are rich in fatty omega-3 acids, like fish, as these can support your brain is having an easier time creating new neural pathways. Some studies suggest that this may make it easier for you to be more resilient toward anxiety and more effective in implementing your new CBT practices.

Use Calming Teas and Herbs

Just like certain herbs can stimulate you, others can actually help you relax, too. Learning how to use tea and herbs to support you in relaxing yourself can be helpful in allowing you to bring down your energy levels and offset your anxiety naturally. Some people like to drink calming teas on a regular basis, whereas others might drink them exclusively around the time that they are feeling anxious so that they can experience relief. Ideally, you should drink calming teas on an ongoing basis. However, either method will support you in naturally bringing down your energy levels and calming yourself from anxiety.

There are seven incredible natural loose leaf teas you can use that will really help you when it comes to bringing down your anxiety levels. These seven include peppermint tea, chamomile tea, lemon balm tea, passionflower tea, green tea, rose tea, and lavender tea. Each of these is known for having various constituents in it that can help you naturally relieve yourself of anxiety, while often also supporting you in uplifting any depression that you may be experiencing.

When it comes to drinking teas or using herbs to support you in navigating anxiety, it is important that you are aware of which ones might worsen your symptoms. Many teas contain higher levels of caffeine, which may or may not offset your anxiety. Some people can handle lightly caffeinated teas, whereas other people might find themselves feeling far too sensitive to even small amounts of caffeine. You can test to see where you fall on this scale. With that being said, avoid black teas and Pu-erh teas as they are known for having more caffeine than coffee, which can make them terrible for managing anxiety. White tea, mate, green tea, and oolong tea can all be used instead of caffeinated beverages and may be gentle enough that they do not stimulate your anxiety, but they do give you a slight boost in energy.

Try Aromatherapy

Aromatherapy has been said to be a powerful tool for helping navigate many different ailments, including anxiety. If you are experiencing troubling anxiety, using aromatherapy may help you support yourself in lowering your anxiety levels and supporting yourself with feeling more at peace in your life. When using aromatherapy, there are a few things that you should know to make sure that you get the most out of your experience while also staying safe.

The first thing you need to know is that aromatherapy works on two levels. The first level is by infusing the constituents of the oil with your body, meaning that it works similarly to tea. The same way that certain elements of tea encourage you to relax in the way that certain elements of aromatherapy blends will encourage you to relax, too. The other way that aromatherapy can help you is through olfaction. Olfaction is a process whereby you smell something, and it activates a part of your limbic system, which essentially means that it triggers certain memories. When certain aromatherapy blends have the capacity to activate your more peaceful memories, it can support you with navigating anxiety more effectively.

Before you begin using aromatherapy, make sure that you purchase your oils from a high-quality source that you trust completely. As well, make sure that you are aware of what oils are safe and are not safe for you to use. Sometimes, essential oils can be dangerous for certain people with certain conditions or for pets, so you need to make sure that the oils you use are safe for yourself and everyone in your home. If you find that the oil you want to use is not safe, do not use it at all as it can cause problems for you or the members of your family rather quickly.

The oils that you can consider using to support you with navigating anxiety include lavender oil, rose oil, vetiver oil, ylang-ylang oil, frankincense oil, geranium oil, jasmine oil, and chamomile oil. All eight of these are known for supporting people with reducing their symptoms of anxiety and experiencing greater calm and peace in their lives.

Release the Pressure From Yourself

The last and sometimes most powerful thing you can do for yourself when you are dealing with anxiety and trying to overcome it naturally releases the pressure for yourself. As a species, we have a tendency to put a massive amount of pressure on ourselves through the expectations that we tend to have on ourselves in life. You may be combining your own high expectations with the expectations that other people have of you, leading to you overwhelming yourself with expectations that you cannot meet. If you are overwhelmed by the expectations that you have placed on yourself, or that you feel others have placed on you, you need to practice taking the pressure off and giving yourself space for a while.

Releasing the pressure from yourself can be difficult, especially if you have had high expectations of yourself for quite some time. You might find yourself struggling to fully release the pressure and let yourself be patient and gentle with yourself, even if you have set the intention to do so. In this case, exercising the practice of CBT on your tendency to put pressure on yourself may be ideal as you learn to change your perspective and give yourself permission to slow down in life and take some of the stuff off of your plate.

The more you can be gentle and patient with yourself, the more you are going to find yourself experiencing peace from your anxiety. Many people are surprised to learn that when they stop expecting so much of themselves, suddenly they have a lot more energy to get everything done. Expectations themselves have a way of slowing people down and making them feel exhausted. If you never take the time to address this, you are going to find yourself constantly feeling overwhelmed and overworked. Learn to take the pressure off of yourself and give yourself permission to take it easy. Book time off, stop saying yes to everything, and delegate some of your tasks so that you do not have to attempt to do so much by yourself. The more you can work on navigating things in a less stressful manner, the less pressure you are going to feel, and therefore the less anxiety you are likely going to feel, too.

Manage Excessive Anger

How often do you feel furious yet don't have a clue why? How regularly do you become forceful and make statements you don't generally mean, and afterward feel agitated and remorseful a short time later? Comparative occasions happen to the majority of us, sooner or later, and we neglect to comprehend the reasons.

Regularly, the appropriate response has to do with extreme weight that has caused you stress, which has gone to outrage as you understand that you seem to have lost control of the circumstance. At that point, you take that outrage and dissatisfaction out on others around you. Now and then that might be your family, or if at work, your associates.

Low confidence, notwithstanding stress, can likewise be at the core of a furious upheaval. You may not recognize this factor, and it is just when you begin to endure the outcomes of that low self-esteem that you may start to investigate the main driver inside yourself.

Losing control is only one way that low confidence shows itself in your conduct. "Why me? It's not reasonable!" is a typical furious upheaval for those experiencing low confidence and sentiment of regularly being the unfortunate casualty in specific conditions.

At the point when we become furious, we moved toward becoming overwhelmed by seen foul play, and afterward, we lose our emphasis on the main thing. At work, we may feel as though we are picked-upon, and in our connections, we may see a shortcoming in others where none truly exists. Maybe we see life through a red dimness - a fog that is outrage.

Defusing Anger

Defusing personal resentment may require the assistance of an expert advisor. However, you can also call upon an esteemed companion who is a decent audience and who will empower you to talk through your anger. That can be done regardless of whether it involves some yelling or crying in disappointment. Drawing out what you feel away from any detectable hindrance is a fantastic technique for looking at your attitude and your disappointment.

Once in a while, getting to the underlying driver of outrage and investigating low confidence issues, requires time and tolerance. Low confidence frequently comes from youth occasions at home or school. Absence of applause and disparagement are essential wellsprings of low confidence, in adolescence. Having the option to place them into setting and managing the resentment that has developed over numerous years is basic.

Outrage can be a risky and unsatisfactory feeling, particularly in the working environment. It can prompt upheavals of anger that could end in brutality, and if your conduct truly ends up troublesome and unsuitable, you can wind up losing your employment.

These are my preferred outrage, the executive's tips:

- If you feel yourself beginning to lose control and you need to yell at somebody, attempt to leave the circumstance. On the off chance that you, at that point, do some profound breathing activities for at any rate five minutes, in a calm spot, you will feel your displeasure begin to scatter. You should then attempt to excuse why you were so angry and afterward come back to what you were doing in advance.

- We all will think we are in every case right, in any event, when we are off-base! The arrangement is to allow others to express their assessments: to effectively tune in to what is being said and afterward to utilize levelheaded discourse to analyze the contention as opposed to losing control and yelling. I realize this is regularly simpler said than done. It takes practice; however, it works.

- In gatherings, be aware that raised voices can rapidly prompt clash. Monitor your sentiments - know about your non-verbal communication - outrage is effectively transmitted through activities and outward appearance, just as proper words.

- Before any passionate upheaval, tally to ten, and when you arrive, you may have diffused the displeasure within yourself.

Nonetheless, if there is an example of angry upheavals, for example, every day, at that point, this likely could be an ideal opportunity to look for proficient restorative counsel as your body may have an unevenness that expects tests to learn the reason. In any case, don't disregard it.

To deal with your annoyance successfully, there will be many things you'll have to think about first. Above all, it is crucial to understand that blowing up is really ordinary and in some cases, even sound. It is the point at which you begin to go overboard to circumstances and lash out at individuals in destructive manners, both to yourself as well as other people, that it turns into an issue. This article will give you some various approaches to take care of this issue and in the long run, become a specialist at controlling your feelings in some random circumstance you are in.

The initial step you will need to take is to distinguish those circumstances and individuals that make it hard to control your anger. At the point when you do this, you will be focusing on those occasions that make you the most troubled, so you can think of successful techniques for dealing with your outrage. You must understand that you will always be unable to dispense with sentiments of anger from your life. Yet, you will have the option to, in the end, control yourself totally and decrease the recurrence of those minutes when you become disturbed and angry.

At the point when you have a rundown of various approaches to monitoring yourself, it is simpler for you to deal with different circumstances that typically aggravate you. On the off chance that one strategy doesn't work, you can attempt another. It's significant that you consider and practice whatever the number of these as could reasonably be expected, so when the crucial point in time of truth shows up, you will have the option to control yourself.

Certain breathing activities have been demonstrated to have any effect when you are losing control. Taking long and full breaths flood oxygen into the body and send it to your cerebrum, making a quieting vibe that will assist you with managing your feelings when you sense that you have no power over them. Significantly, you practice these also with the goal for them to be as viable as conceivable at helping you deal with your resentment.

It is better at that point to prevent this to outrage from emerging in any case - by adequately 'dealing with our displeasure' - by remaining quiet, so we don't get to this phase of the annoyance cycle. In this article, I will accordingly give some straightforward; however, compelling procedures for remaining quiet that can be used in many circumstances.

Strategies to Cope with Immediate Stress and Anger

Leave THE SOURCE OF ANGER: By remaining close to any wellspring of stress and outrage, frequently include more pressure and outrage without us doing anything. That can be an individual, item, or circumstance causing the resentment and can be in any condition from home, work environment, or on our day by day ventures. If at all conceivable, my best counsel is to attempt to expel ourselves from this pressure. It may mean pardoning oneself from the circumstance; for example, if the load is being brought about by a relative during supper, we could forgive ourselves and leave the room before getting excessively irate. In a working environment circumstance, it may be the case that the report we have been composing for as far back as two hours is turning out badly. Rather than battling further while tired and committing more errors - just adding to the pressure; we could have a break, either by leaving the workplace, getting an espresso - or if this is beyond imagination even basically sitting at the PC and having a speedy look at the web for a couple of moments to loosen up ourselves.

Quiet DOWN BY USING DEEP BREATHING: One of the indications of expanded pressure and outrage is a reviving of the breath brought about by expanded pulse, prompting the blood requiring more oxygen, requiring snappier breath - and in that capacity the cycle proceeds. By breathing gradually, we can break this cycle and enable ourselves to quiet down. The procedure here is to take long full breaths in through the nose, hold these for a second and afterward remove a long full breath from the mouth for a few seconds, rehashing the cycle for a while. This timespan changes relying upon how focused on we are yet additionally to what extent we need to play out this action. The facts may confirm that we have the opportunity to do this in the lift before we meet someone, so twenty seconds might be all we have. At the opposite finish of the scale, we may have 10-15 or more minutes to extra. Regardless of to what extent, doing this in any event, for a couple of moments, can help offer some relief from the resentment and for longer than a couple of moments can significantly diminish individual feelings of anxiety.

Envision A RELAXING EXPERIENCE WE HAVE HAD OR SOMETHING CALMING: When feeling pushed, envision a circumstance in the past where we have felt loose, can help loosen up our brain. Additionally, pondering nothing at all can likewise be similarly as compelling, if not more so. When doing this, attempt to not consider anything by any stretch of the imagination

- something that sounds simple yet marginally progressively hard to do practically speaking. Effectively utilizing both these systems takes practice, yet once accomplished, the outcomes can be powerful. For sure, in the same way as other 'quieting' procedures, these are best when used in calm spots: it can be at our work area when the workplace is vacant, or sitting on the transport to and from work, or having a stroll along the road when alone. It abandons saying that this strategy ought not to be used when we require full focus or when we are in a domain where we should be alert.

Long haul Techniques

The following arrangement of methods for quieting us is 'long haul.' By this, I mean progressing things that we can do to constrain pressure and outrage - to prevent these from working up in any case by accomplishing certain items over a more drawn out timeframe.

Ensure THAT WE GET REGULAR EXERCISE AND A HEALTHY BALANCED DIET: Regular exercise isn't fundamental for our physical wellbeing and prosperity yet additionally for our emotional wellness. Practice enables our mind to create more dopamine (a natural stimulant), which thus helps our state of mind and makes us feel more joyful. Taking customary exercise at that point helps our general state of mind incredibly. Taking approximately 30 minutes of activity - including strolling at a quick pace-every day can enormously confine our pressure and outrage levels while making us more advantageous physically. Consolidate this with a sound adjusted eating routine, and the outcomes can be much increasingly excellent. While it is past the transmit of this article to go into diet and which nourishments ought to be eaten and in what amounts, guidance for this exists in numerous different spots. Doing this can have a checked effect upon by, and substantial feelings of anxiety and can keep us physically more beneficial all the while.

Attempt TO GET A GOOD NIGHT SLEEP: This most likely sounds clear, yet I will state it at any rate. A decent night rest (ideally 7-9 hours for grown-ups) and around 9-10 hours for kids are prescribed for general wellbeing. It helps me to remember a familiar saying I once found out about resting times, 'commonly 5, by custom 7, by apathy 9 and insidiousness 11'. We are, for the most part, people and have our very own favored length of rest. While it is difficult in our bustling lives to get 8 hours of the night - and considerably increasingly hard for kids, particularly in their high school years-for us all, it is fundamental that we get these prescribed long stretches of rest every night. Similarly significant is that we get into an ordinary resting design. By getting our full amount of rest, we will be increasingly conscious during the day, less drained and in that capacity have improved fixation, all prompting less pressure and outrage.

Attempt TO HAVE PERSONAL RELATION TIME EVERY DAY: Again, this is something hard to accomplish in our bustling day by day plans, yet taking even 20-30 minutes out of every day to accomplish something that we appreciate can assist (a) with relaxing our psyche and (b) with going about as a stimulant enabling us to feel more joyful. We may think that we are too occupied to even think about taking this break, feeling that we are progressively beneficial accomplishing different things. While this might be valid, by not having this unwinding 'switch-off' time over a time of days, we just become increasingly worn out and less gainful - prompting things not be done appropriately, not getting round to tasks and accordingly getting to be pushed. That thus can promptly provoke displeasure.

BE Organized AND TRY NOT TO LET THINGS BUILD-UP: This is the last suggestion I am going to give here. Being sorted out is the bedrock of casual life. Disorder - regardless of whether this is through leaving bills unpaid, beginning for work past the point of no return, or being late for arrangements all lead to abrupt undesirable pressure and outrage - harming our wellbeing yet having a dramatic and contrary effect on our own and business relations. My best exhortation is to attempt to keep awake to date with everything from administrative work: accounts: arrangements and leave an abundant measure of time for doing these exercises. Sometimes, in order to maintain a distance from stress, we have to go out 20 minutes sooner or commit a particular day at regular intervals to sort out our accounts. Whatever this might be, we must remain composed to battle life stresses and the subsequent displeasure these can bring.

Like there is a day and night the same way, we have different sides to our feelings. There are glad feelings, and there are dim feelings. Dim feelings are a piece of what your identity is, and they give input about what is occurring you throughout everyday life.

We experience different feelings at various times of life. Every emotion works unexpectedly. For instance, dread and outrage invigorate you to activity, though misery and blame go about as depressants. In case we don't express or address these feelings, they will develop to the point of wild ejection. On the off chance that you harbor outrage inside you, you will undoubtedly explode the spread one day and lose everything all the while. That is our dim feeling; however, that doesn't mean it shouldn't have been managed.

When you are furious with somebody, you have to express your resentment adequately. It's not generally the most straightforward activity; however, it's the correct method to channel your annoyance and accomplish positive outcomes out of an adverse circumstance.

First, you ought to comprehend the contrast between grumble and analysis. In case you have an issue with your partner, or any other person, it's critical to know how you are going to deal with it. The analysis leaves the other individual inclination genuinely charged and guarded, which incites them to assault you back. The endless loop or assaults will begin, and you won't have the option to pass on the point you at first began to, and it might make you much angrier and progressively disappointed.

There are unquestionably issues in the majority of our lives that are difficult to manage, and we may require some outside help in achieving them. Outrage is one that undoubtedly hangs out in my brain. It's a terrible passionate response to something that makes us feel awful, agitated, baffled, and an entire slew of different things that we more often than do whatever it takes not to stay away from in regular daily existence. The significant thing here is to recall that you aren't the only one, and we will cover approaches to deal with your resentment, so it doesn't oversee you.

Outrage is communicated through a wide range of means extremely subject to the individual or individual doing the communication. A few of us are unquestionably more significant at managing outrage than others. A few of us are ready to get it off our chests by conversing with a companion or relative, while others brush it off and attempt to remain concentrated on other significant exercises.

The significant thing secured above is managing outrage with regards to other individuals. How precisely we are communicating it to other individuals is the worry. If it is through general discussion, that is a specific something, however, when we start to take it out on others is the point at which the connection is crossed, and an adverse action is then occurring.

You can certainly do something specific to help with controlling your outrage and the methods in which you express it. If you imagine that you have an annoying issue that you can only with significant effort oversee, then it is unquestionably prescribed to look for advising. Advising ought to never be taken as an awful choice if you imagine that it is in certainty good.

Cognitive Behavioral Treatments for Anxiety and Depression

Treating Anxiety Disorders with Therapy

It doesn't matter whether you are suffering from an incapacitating phobia, panic attacks, unrelenting worries or obsessive thoughts, what is more, important is that you don't have to live a life full of anxiety and fear. Anxiety and fear be treated. Therapy is the most effective option for your anxiety problem. The reason why anxiety therapy is the best option is that it differs from other anxiety medication in many ways. Anxiety therapy focuses on treating anxiety beyond just symptoms of the problem because it uncovers the main underlying causes of your fears and worries; and then teaches you how to overcome these worries and fears. Anxiety therapy will teach you how to relax, how to look at a situation from a different perspective and in less frightening ways and in the end, you will be able to develop skills on how to cope and solve your problems. In other words, therapy will give you the best tools for overcoming anxiety as well as teach you how to use these tools.

Anxiety therapy should always be tailored towards the specific symptoms and diagnosis a particular patient presents. Usually, the length depends on the severity level of a patient's social anxiety disorder. Many anxiety therapies, as observed by the American Psychological Association, are usually relatively short-term, and most people tend to indicate significant improvements within eight therapeutic sessions. Their several therapies approach for treating social anxiety and the leading approaches to treating social anxiety are Metacognitive Therapy (MCT) and Cognitive Behavioural Therapy (CBT). We can use each of these anxiety therapy treatments separately or by combining them with other therapeutic approaches. Basically, anxiety therapy can be done either to an individual or to a group of individuals having the same anxiety problems. Irrespective of the anxiety therapy chosen, the goal still remains the same; lowering your anxiety level, overcome your fears, and calm your mind.

CBT (Cognitive Behavioral Therapy)

This therapy is best-preferred approach and widely adopted for the treatment of anxiety disorders. Most researches have shown that CBT is a very effective therapeutic approach for treating social anxiety disorder and panic disorder. Basically, Cognitive behavioral therapy focused on addressing the negative thought patterns and thought distortions that affect the way we perceive ourselves and the world around us. Just as suggested by its name, CBT consists of two main components

1. Cognitive therapy: Cognitive therapy focuses on examining how our negative thoughts make us anxious.

2. Behavior therapy: Behavior therapy focuses on how an individual responds to or behaves when faced with anxiety triggering situations.

CBT bases itself on the fact that the way we feel is determined by how we think and not by external events. This means that the situation you are in does not determine your feelings. How you feel (your feelings) are determined by how you perceive the situation you are in. Here is a case where you have been invited to a big party. In mind, you are thinking about this invitation in different ways. As you think, there are emotions you will have.

First thought: This party is going to have a lot of fun. I just love it because there will be many people and I will make new friends.

Your emotions: You will feel eager, excited and happy

Second thought: I generally don't like parties. I prefer to have to stay indoors and watch some movies or code.

Your Emotions: Neutral

Third Thought: I have never been to a party; what will I do when told to speak or when told to dance. I also don't know how to dress. People will laugh at me.

Your Emotions: You will feel sad or anxious.

Clearly, these three thoughts can make an individual have three different emotions. Our emotions depend on what we believe in, attitudes, and individual expectations. More often, individuals with anxiety disorders have a negative manner of thinking, and actually, this is what propagates negative emotions which in turn yields to fear and anxiety. Cognitive-behavioral therapy for anxiety has the main goal of identifying and correcting the negative beliefs and thoughts that a person with an anxiety disorder has. Cognitive-behavioral therapy bases its treatment on ensuring that you change your ways of thought as one way of changing how you feel.

- CBT will teach you how to recognize when you are anxious and how that makes your body feel

- CBT will teach you coping skills as well as techniques to use so as to feel relaxed as one way of countering panic and anxiety.

- CBT will teach you how to confront your fears both in real life and in your imaginations.

Metacognitive Therapy (MCT)

In almost our daily activities, there are times that we are overwhelmed by negative thoughts, and we tend to believe in these negative thinking. However, it is not everyone who develops sustained anxiety, emotional suffering, or depression. Therefore, I would like to begin by asking yourself, what it that controls your thoughts is and what is it that determines whether you can dismiss these thoughts or what is it that makes these thoughts sink in and make you have even a prolonged and deeper distress.

We will try to offer an answer to these questions by looking at metacognition. Both healthy and unhealthy controls of the mind are based on metacognition. Metacognition bases on principle that; an individual's emotions and the control over these emotions are not determined by what a person thinks about is determined by how a person thinks. Let's look at thinking like some large orchestra activity which has many players and many instruments. In such a case, an acceptable overture can only be produced when there are a conductor and a music score. Therefore, in the human mind, metacognition is the conductor and the score behind thinking. In other words, we can say that metacognition is like cognition to cognition. Metacognition is responsible for controlling, monitoring, and appraising your awareness.

Emotional discomfort is transitory in most people because they have learned flexible ways with which they can deal with negative thoughts and beliefs constructed by their minds. The metacognitive approach bases on the idea that we become trapped in our emotional disturbance due to the fact that our metacognitions causes e a particular pattern with which we respond to our inner experiences responsible for maintaining our emotions and strengthening of the negative ideas we have. The pattern that should, therefore, be looked into is the cognitive attentional syndrome (CAS). This pattern consists of fixated attention, worry, unhelpful coping behaviors, unhelpful strategies for self-regulation, and ruminations.

Metacognitive therapy bases on the principle that metacognition plays a critical role in the understanding of the operation of cognition and how cognition generates the conscious experiences that people have for themselves and the world around them. Metacognition is responsible for shaping what we pay attention to as well as the factors that enter our consciousness. Metacognition is also responsible for shaping our appraisals and influencing the different strategies we have to adopt while regulating our thoughts and feelings.

The nature of metacognitive therapy

Metacognition basically describes a range of interrelating factors which consists of cognitive process or any knowledge involved in the control of monitoring, interpretation, and control of cognition. Metacognitive therapy is therefore divided into three; exploring knowledge and beliefs, exploring experiences and then coming up with effective strategies.

i. Knowledge and Beliefs

Metacognitive therapy begins by examining the beliefs and theories that people tend to have in their thoughts. We are in a society where some thoughts or actions are linked to some beliefs. For example, there are cases where you may feel that your religion does not allow you to have some thoughts as that would lead you to punishment because they are such thoughts are sinful. These are some of the beliefs that will affect your thoughts if you hold on to them. Metacognitive therapy will exploit two types of metacognitive knowledge; first, we will exploit your explicit or declarative beliefs and secondly, we will exploit your implicit or procedural beliefs. Implicit and procedural knowledge basically represents an individual's thinking skills.

a. Explicit knowledge

This is what you can express verbally. For example, you can say. "If I continue to be with this worry, I will get depressed and may have even had a heart attack.";" I don't like the way they looked at me and laugh. I think they are seeing me as incapable." Therefore, a patient will be asked to try to express all his worries verbally to be noted.

b. Implicit knowledge

This type of knowledge cannot be expressed verbally. They can be seen as the programs or rules guiding how we think. For instance, implicit knowledge guides things like allocation of attention, use of heuristics when coming up with judgments and memory search.

c. Positive metacognitive beliefs

These are beliefs that are associated with thoughts that benefit an individual. In this case, an individual need to examine all his positive thoughts and focus his/her attention on them. For example, one can say that "Worrying about the coming exam will make me read, and when I read, I will pass my exams."

d. Negative metacognitive beliefs

These are beliefs that are associated with uncontrollability, and such beliefs will make an individual have dangerous thoughts relating to feeling worthless. For example, one can have dangerous thoughts like " I am wondering how of late I can't remember names, I think I have a brain tumor."

ii. Experiences

Metacognitive experiences focus on exploring situations that changed an individual's feelings on his/her mental status. Experiences are based on an individual's subjective feelings. In Metacognitive therapy attempts to control an individual's thinking, particularly the thoughts that raise the negative appraisals of feelings. Strategies

iii. Metacognitive strategies

Metacognitive strategies provide the best responses for controlling and altering an individual's thinking in relation to the regulation of emotions and cognition. These strategies focus on suppressing or changing the nature of an individual's cognitive activities. Negative emotions and thoughts can be reduced by altering some aspects of cognition. In this way, an individual can be made to have positive thoughts as one way of distracting or suppressing the distressing thoughts and emotions.

Adopting the Metacognitive Model of GAD

For normal people, negative thoughts are things that come and go and will not raise any negative response that will, in turn, affect them. However, there are people who when they have negative thoughts, they end up having worrying. General anxiety disorder model tries to help such individuals avoid such thoughts, anticipate the problems related to such thoughts, or find a solution to such thoughts. We look at about an individual's worry on physical self, social, and world. The metacognitive model of GAD tries to link worrying to positive metacognitive beliefs. In most cases, despite people worrying occasionally, many people have positive beliefs in relation to worrying. The metacognitive model, however, makes an assumption that self-regulation and emotional problems can be caused by over-reliance on worry as a way of trying to respond to negative thinking. Therefore, worrying can significantly contribute to a non-specific vulnerability on your emotions. General anxiety disorder develops the moment you start; you start activating and developing negative beliefs. More often, these beliefs are formed when we are exposed to interpretations of internal events or exposed to some information.

How Will Anxiety Therapy Work for You?

Anxiety has no fast solution. You can only be able to overcome an anxiety disorder when you take your time and be committed towards it. You are required to be ready to face your fears rather than avoiding them. Therefore, be ready to feel worse so as to get better. It is important that you stick with the treatment plan and follow the advice of your therapist. There are times that you will almost feel discouraged with your recovery pace maybe because it is taking time. I think one thing you should know is that anxiety therapy is very effective when conducted at a slower pace. Be patient, and you will see the benefits. As an individual, you can focus on supporting your own anxiety therapy by being smart and taking positive steps and choices. Anxiety is affected by everything in you and around you, ranging from your daily activities to social lifestyle. Be a person who is able to make conscious decisions that will make you more relaxed; develop a more positive mental outlook and vitality in your daily life.

It is appropriate that you learn more about anxiety. You cannot overcome a problem without knowing the problem. Advance your knowledge of anxiety. This is where MCT and CBT education is applied. However, education alone is not enough to cure anxiety disorder but rather will play a very important role in ensuring that you fully benefit from the therapy.

Try to promote your connections with other people. Isolation and loneliness create an effective platform for anxiety. Just ensure that you reach to others and socialize more so as to decrease your vulnerability to anxiety. Make new friends, visit them frequently, and choose your loved ones whom you can freely share your concerns and worries with. You can also join support groups or self-help groups.

It is also appropriate that you adopt healthy lifestyle habits. It is advisable that you include physical activity or exercise in your daily activities because this is one way of relieving anxiety tension. Never use stimulants, drugs, and alcohol to enable you to cope with anxiety symptoms as this may even turn worse.

Reduce stress or don't associate with things stressing you. Take your time and examine your life. Identify those thoughts or events that make you feel stressed. Find a solution to those you can and avoid the rest that you cannot. If there are people who make you feel anxious, be ready to avoid them. Also, be bold to say no to extra responsibilities added to you. Always ensure that you make time to relax and have fun.

Maintaining Positive Mindfulness

Mindfulness is the practice of being fully aware of where you are and what you are doing, and not being overwhelmed by the things around you. Every person has the innate capability of being mindful, but it becomes strong when you practice it on a daily basis.

Whenever you develop awareness for what you're doing either through your senses or thoughts and emotions, you are being mindful. Research shows that mindfulness modifies brain structure and improves the quality of our lives.

For a person suffering from depression or anxiety, they have a much better chance of reducing the symptoms by indulging in mindfulness. The following are some tips for practicing mindfulness:

- Set aside some time: start by setting aside some time for practicing mindfulness meditation. The beauty of mindfulness is that you don't have to incur an expense. But you have to allocate some time-resource. This is ideally the time you are most comfortable and are at peace with yourself. You have to honor this schedule no matter what you may be doing.

- Improve your observation skills: mindfulness is about being aware of what's happening around you. Thus, you have to be pretty aware of your surroundings. Ensure that you develop your observation skills so that you can be able to tell what's going on around you. With great observation skills, nothing will escape your notice.

- Let go your judgments: it is in human nature to judge different things that we see. But in this state of mindfulness, you must not let yourself be influenced by your judgments. Just take the role of the observer and watch your judgments go by.

- Fight distractions: there are many instances in which we are distracted by a variety of things. Once distractions come into the scene, they carry your focus away. Thus, you must ensure that you have laser focus, and keep your mind to the present moment.

- Notice your contributions: learn to recognize the role you play in your environment. By identifying the things that are as a result of your doings, it strengthens your power of introspection.

Mindfulness exercises for anxiety and depression

The following mindfulness exercises are aimed at helping a person overcome their anxiety:

1. Mindfulness breathing

This exercise is perhaps the commonest exercise in mindfulness. It is very effective in eliminating distress, and fighting both anxiety and depression. The beauty of this exercise is that virtually anyone can practice it, and all you have to do is find somewhere peaceful for your daily ritual. You can also perform the exercise quickly whenever you are overwhelmed. It starts by assuming a comfortable position. Some people might stand, sit by a window, or even lie on a bed. You are the one that knows what position is most comfortable. Once you get into that position, close your eyes, and put both hands on your chest. And then you may begin to breathe in and out slowly. As you expel your breath, ensure that you focus on your thoughts, and resist the urge to fight the bad thoughts. This act alone is enough to get rid of the bad emotions and fears.

2. The raisin exercises

This exercise is performed at the introductory stages. It basically tests various senses of an individual. Anyone can perform this exercise. It starts with putting a raisin in front of you and observing a variety of things:

- How it looks
- How it feels
- How it smells
- How it tastes

By focusing on the raisin, you are in a position to bring your mind to the present moment.

3. The body scans

This is another exercise that doesn't require much in order to perform. First off, the participant must lie on their back, with their palms facing up, and their feet held slightly apart. In that state, the participant may be still, listening to the sensations of their body, and paying attention to how their skin feels against different things. They may take a deep breath and expel the breath in slight gasps, exploring the contents of their mind. The participant uses either palm alternately to scan various parts of their body while they "listen" to the sensations that are elicited.

4. Mindful seeing

Vision plays a big role in the art of mindfulness. Thus, it necessitates this exercise. Mindful seeing heightens a person's awareness and helps them understand their present reality. It starts with sitting by a window and looking out, where there's the light of a city. Start looking at the different things that are emitting lights in the city and fight the urge to label them. By allowing yourself to notice all these lights, you will relieve yourself of emotional burdens and getting started to conquer your anxiety and depression.

5. Mindfulness watching your thoughts

The average person has many thoughts coasting through their mind at any given time. Some thoughts can pass by and they won't be aware. But when you engage in mindfulness watching of your thoughts, you are in a position to understand how your brain works. Start off by assuming a comfortable position, preferably a lying position, facing up the ceiling. You can put on some soothing instrumental music for effect. Then close your eyes and start watching your thoughts. Fight the urge to label those thoughts and take the role of the observer. This exercise will not only relieve you of anxiety and depression but it will help you understand how you perceive various things.

6. Mindfulness preparation for sleep

The problem with having anxiety or depression is that it takes away a person's ability to fall asleep quickly. The affected person might jump into bed but they will stay awake for a very long time. But thanks to mindfulness, you actually have a chance to sleep as fast as you would hope. It starts with you taking a shower and putting on your sleeping clothes and then climbing atop your bed with your eyes facing up. Focus on the ceiling above and envision your mind as an empty vessel. Slowly, start filling up your mind with light, and watch as the vessel slowly gets filled up with whiteness. It will create a hypnotized sensation that will promptly put you to sleep.

Powerful Steps to Self-Love

Most of us have grown up thinking that we need others to love who we are so that we can be happy. Wanting others to love you is no bad goal. However, if you're going to stop at nothing in order to be loved, if you're going to let others have their way at your expense, then that's unfair to yourself—and ultimately, you're going to be mad at both yourself and the world. Self-love is treating yourself as you would a good friend. It is about satisfying your needs and forgiving yourself. Self-love is associated with the following:

Low Anxiety

Depression

More Happiness

More Optimism

Healthy Habits

Happiness

The following are some of the practices that boost self-love:

Start Your Day on a Positive Note

Start your day by telling yourself something that will put a smile on your face. When you hit your day off on a positive note, you get to take on other activities of the day with a positive mindset. You can start the day by reminding yourself of how well you handled a situation, the important role that you play in someone's life or in a company, and so on.

Eat Healthy Foods

Research has shown that there's a correlation between the foods we eat and our emotional state. If we eat unhealthy foods, such as junk foods, we are more likely to be stressed out and anxious as compared to if we eat a meal consisting of nutritious ingredients. Food is our fuel. For the optimal functioning of our body, we need to consume food that will nourish us, and provide us with the energy to complete various tasks. Healthy meals encourage us to cook our meals at home, instead of eating out, thus saving money.

Workout

The more fit you are, the more likely you are to experience happy feelings and have high self-esteem. But if your body is in terrible shape, you are likely to suffer low self-esteem, and it will contribute to making poor decisions. Get into the habit of working out regularly. The following are some of the benefits associated with exercising:

Improved Heart Health

Improved Blood Circulation

Improved Brain Health

Improved Sleep Quality

Improved Moods

There are various ways, both expensive and inexpensive, to get started on working out.

Silence Your Inner Critic

There's an inner critic inside each one of us that complicates things. This critic is harsh on us and makes us feel terrible. We should make a point of silencing this critic before they do us major harm. But this doesn't mean we should ignore any form of criticism.

Surround Yourself with Positive People

They say that a person is the average of the five people they spend the most time with. True. Make a point of spending time with only positive individuals. This will make you take on their positive traits and help you become better at making decisions.

Stop Comparing Yourself with Others

There will always be people more successful and less successful than you. But more importantly, success can adhere to your own definition. Have your own idea of success. Comparing yourself to other people will take away your self-worth when you come up short.

Cut Off Toxic People

Toxic people are nothing more than energy vampires. They will steal away your positive energy and leave you feeling terrible. Make a point of getting rid of them. Of course, it is not easy to distance yourself from toxic people – especially if you have been the energy supply – but take baby steps first, like refusing to hang out with them, and then large steps like changing residence.

Celebrate Your Wins

There's nothing like "a small win." If you make a step forward, always get into a celebratory mood. Being grateful to yourself will allow you to tap into the whole of your potential. Winning in small ways will instill a winning mindset into your subconscious, and you are far more likely to achieve most of your goals.

Step Out of Your Comfort Zone

As long as you're in your comfort zone, you will never know what you're really capable of. Push yourself out of your comfort zone and watch your life turn around.

Success is always found in the extra effort that we apply. If you are looking for a life partner, try to meet more people, instead of locking yourself away and complaining that there are no suitable partners.

Embrace Your Quirkiness

If you have some traits that are considered "out of the norm," you should embrace them, instead of being ashamed of them. If you stand tall with your quirkiness, you will draw people in. There will be a sense of uniqueness about you.

Follow Your Passion

It's the one thing that excites you, but at the same time, you're scared of failing. Overcome your fear of failure and go for your passion. Many successful people have revealed that their secret to success is merely following what they are most passionate about.

Help Others

By helping others, we get a huge sense of fulfillment. It is incredibly satisfying to lighten the burden of other people. It is also a form of networking. Life is interconnected. At one point, you may require something and find yourself needing the expertise of the person that you helped, in which case it will be rendered easily.

Strengthen Your Relationships

You're not resourceful enough to stay on your own. You will always depend on others, particularly your life partner. Work on strengthening your close relationships so that you can enjoy abundant peace of mind and support.

Give Up the Need for the Approval of Others

No matter what you do, there will always be someone to find fault with it. Desist from trying to be in everyone's good book. Think about it; when everyone likes you, you won't have anyone to prove yourself to, and your success will be kind of bland. Do you know why Sylvester Stallone feels so great about himself? It's because he received a lot of rejection before he finally got his breakthrough. And now he feels great knowing that all those executives that shunned him have helplessly seen him become a star.

Conclusion

Now you have reached the end of this book, but not the end of your CBT journey. These pages have prepared you to use CBT to transform your mind and consequently your life. That does not mean that your journey is over; rather, it has just begun. CBT is your best friend. It is a companion that you should carry with you through the rest of your life. Keep using it to see marked changes in how you approach life and how you feel.

Here is a wrap up of everything covered in this book:

Avoiding situations that bring you harm is great. But in real life, we both know that that is not always realistic. Life throws plenty of bad situations at you and you can't avoid them all. Therefore, it is essential to develop healthy coping skills for when you do encounter these situations.

Situations that stir up mental illness symptoms can be everyday situations that other, healthier people find to be no big deal. But for you, they can feel catastrophic. They can lead you to relapse in your symptoms, after working so hard to overcome those symptoms with CBT. Learning to cope in harmful everyday situations is essential to keep yourself from falling into despair.

Anxiety

Many everyday situations that are nothing to healthy people can trigger severe anxiety in some. For instance, a huge crowd at an airport can be stressful for anyone, but it can be disastrous for you if you have agoraphobia or social anxiety. But what if you have to fly for work or to visit a sick relative? You have to be a part of that airport crowd, whether you like it or not. The situation is not ideal for you but you can use various techniques to cope with your anxiety.

The best technique is relaxation. Focus on your breathing. Breathe in through your nose, out through your mouth. By focusing on your breathing, you take your mind off of the stress that surrounds it.

Progressive muscle relaxation also is helpful in anxiety-provoking situations. Start first from the muscles in your scalp. Force yourself to relax those muscles. Next move to your forehead muscles. Keep roving your mind over your body, forcing the relaxation of each of your muscle groups. The relaxation will calm you and the intense mental focus required to perform this exercise will take your mind off of your stress.

Some people find tapping to be soothing. You can repeat a mantra to yourself such as, "I will survive this. This is really not so bad" as you tap different parts of your body. The physical action of tapping paired with the repeated affirmation can help trick your mind into believing what you are saying to yourself.

Sometimes anxiety can impair your ability to focus on anything. In that case, it is essential to pick a spot on the wall and focus on it intently. Do not chase any other thoughts that enter your head. That spot on the wall is your refuge. Use it to take your mind off of the craziness raging around you and within you.

Facing Your Fears

CBT is great for helping you overcome irrational fears and phobias. This is because CBT allows you to think about your phobias and understand that they are not rational and not conducive to your peace of mind.

If you have a phobia, you may find it very helpful to write about your phobia. When it is on paper, you will begin to see how silly it really is. If you are scared of airplanes, what are the odds of a crash, really? You are far more likely to die in a car crash than a plane crash.

If you are scared of dogs because of a traumatic encounter with a dog in your childhood, remember that most dogs are man's best friends and that you are a lot bigger now. Analyze your fears to see how scary they really are.

To truly overcome your phobia, you need to begin to condition yourself to it. Exposing yourself to what scares you can help teach your mind to stop fearing it as it witnesses you emerge unscathed. There are classes you can take to condition yourself to overcome fear of heights, flying, and other phobias. Consider going to the snake or spider exhibit at a local zoo to stand near the creatures that make you want to scream. You will begin to realize that your phobias do not hurt you. If you have social phobia, try taking brief walks outside and striking up a brief conversation with one stranger a day.

The above relaxation techniques can also really help you when you are feeling the vise grip of fear from a phobia. Breathe, focus, and use progressive muscle relaxation to bring yourself out of your fear.

Handling Depression

The hardest part of coping with depression is that depression cripples your will to do anything. You may not even have the energy to get out of bed, let alone perform CBT on yourself. But coping with your depression gets easier when you begin to change your thinking to more positive thoughts. Positive thinking has the ability to release feel-good hormones like serotonin in your brain, allowing you to feel better and begin to move forward with your life.

When you find yourself drowning in depression symptoms, there may be a reason that you feel so blue. Maybe life is just hard right now or you have not been taking care of your body. Try to identify the source of your depression and remove it from your life. Focus on the present and enjoying life right now. Life is too short to be spent suffering in your bed.

Anger Management

If you have trouble managing your anger, you need to step back and breathe when you start to see red. Use your CBT journal to write down why a situation made you mad enough to hit someone or have an outburst.

Then, analyze the situation. Was it really what you thought, or were you doing something like assuming and negative labeling? Were you ignoring the positives of the situation, or of a person that angered you? Now, in the future, how can you handle this situation without hitting and throwing things and lashing out verbally? Is there something you can do that is more conducive to a reasonable solution?

Rarely is anger ever a solution. Uncontrolled anger can get you into a lot of trouble with loved ones and even the law. Breathe, and think of better ways to react to situations than angry outbursts.

Using CBT to Overcome addiction

Addiction is often referred to as an illness. Many people fail to understand that addiction is usually a symptom of a deeper illness. People use drugs, alcohol, and other addictive behaviors such as gambling to create instant gratification and numb themselves against life. These addictive behaviors offer addicts temporary pleasure that drowns out the deeper pain addicts are experiencing inside of themselves. Basically, addicts use their addictions to distract themselves, or numb themselves, from what is really wrong. When the pleasure wears off, addicts literally feel like they are in hell because they have no shield from their pain, and they desperately chase a new high or thrill to keep them in the numb, pleased state that lets them ignore their problems. Addicts often live in denial of their real problems, and engage in harmful behaviors to avoid feeling the emotional fallout from their life situations, past traumas, or their childhoods.

Since CBT can address inner thoughts and thus change outer behaviors, it offers a rich opportunity for addicts to overcome their addictions. Addicts can use CBT to identify the thoughts and emotions that drive them to use and replace those thoughts and emotions with healthier ones that do not drive them to seek numbness. It also helps them learn to avoid situations, also known as triggers, which lead to relapses. In addition, addicts can use CBT to find healthy alternatives to self-medicating using substances, shopping, gambling, eating, sex, or whatever vice they have chosen to escape their problems with.

Identify addictive behaviors and the thoughts behind them. If you suddenly crave a drug, what triggered you to want to use? Was it a tense situation, like an argument with your family or a rough day at work? Did you see someone or hear a song from your drug days that made your brain start thinking about drugs?

Now, think of better ways to cope with the current situation. Maybe you can do yoga or exercise to relieve stress. Maybe just writing in your journal and taking a hot shower is all you need. Engage in healthy feel-good coping mechanisms, rather than participating in substance use. While substance use can relieve your bad feelings in the short term, it only worsens your mental health and your life circumstances in the long term.

Above all, remember your resolve to be clean and sober. You have made tremendous progress. Your life and your health are probably significantly better without drugs and alcohol playing a role in your behavior. You don't want to backtrack now and discount everything that you have accomplished. One way to deal with cravings and addiction is to remember why you wanted to get clean in the first place.

Remind yourself of the awful things about drug use that made you want to quit.

Then, think about all that you have accomplished in getting clean. You have done something that less than fourteen percent of drug users do.

Lightning Source UK Ltd.
Milton Keynes UK
UKHW010901080223
416610UK00013B/932